# STEALTH JAPAN

# STEALTH
# JAPAN

## THE SURPRISE SUCCESS OF THE
## WORLD'S FIRST INFOMERC ECONOMY

### SCOTT FOSTER

FOREWORD BY MARK ANDERSON

PUBLISHED IN THE UNITED STATES OF AMERICA BY

FiReBooks

A DIVISION OF THE STRATEGIC NEWS SERVICE

SNS | STRATEGIC
NEWS SERVICE

Published in the United States of America by FiReBooks, a division of the Strategic News Service.
P.O. Box 1969
Friday Harbor, Washington 98250
www.stratnews.com

FiRe, FiReBooks, and Strategic News Service (SNS) are registered international trademarks. All other trademarks, servicemarks, registered trademarks, and registered servicemarks are the property of their respective owners.

Ordering Information:
Bookstores and wholesalers should contact the publisher at the address above. Special discounts are available on quantity purchases by corporations, associations, and others. For details, contact the publisher.

The publisher is not responsible for websites (or their content) that are not owned by the publisher.

Cover image © Babak Tafreshi, The World at Night (http://twanight.org)

ISBN (print): 978-0-9967254-2-2
ISBN (ebook): 978-0-9967254-0-8

10 9 8 7 6 5 4 3 2 1

Printed in the United States of America

# Contents

# Foreword

We see countries in many different ways: as places on a map, as players in peace or war, as centers of culture and language, as political systems and their leaders. Almost certainly, one lens most of us do not use – and, it turns out, the one that subsumes all of these other views – is the national business model. Just like companies, every country today has a method for making money, and it is this methodology that most clearly distinguishes one nation from another in the 21st century.

Today, the global economy is driven by technology. It is possible that in the past it was driven by gold, or spices, or energy, or cheap labor – even by a strong navy – but in the post-Information Age there is absolutely no doubt: every sector in the world's economy is driven by technical advances.

For this reason, it isn't hard to understand why the greatest contest between nations today is not between the old "isms" of the cold war or East vs. West, but rather something much simpler. Almost without exception, the world's great nations today fall into one of two categories: those that invent things, creating substantive new technological advances; and those that don't, often incrementally improving on others' major steps forward.

Among these latter countries, the question then becomes: How will they obtain the inventions that drive today's economy? The answers vary. Some nations, such as Japan, have a mixed history, licensing and paying for some intellectual property while copying and reverse-engineering other IP. Some nations, like China, have opted directly for a sophisticated and structured plan for the massive theft of other nations' commercial secrets.

In both cases, these countries are employing a business model that came from the centuries-old "mercantilist" model – perhaps first tried by the British – which does everything possible to favor exports over imports. Brought forward into modern times, Japan has molded its own postwar version of this model around the Information Society. For this reason, we have decided to call this version of the model "InfoMercantilism" – a long word that simply implies that the country is using information (trade secrets) to fuel a model that favors exports over imports.

One cannot over-emphasize the importance of understanding the nature of this intended trade asymmetry in understanding how the Japanese economy works today.

Indeed, the sole function of the InfoMercantilist model, and therefore the sole metric of its success, is the advancement of asymmetrical trade – of exporting more than importing. There are many techniques inside the model that work together to achieve this goal, but the goal itself is almost shockingly simple. The model is not designed, for example, to help the poor, or improve farming, or espouse a certain political view, or keep domestic prices reasonable. In fact, in favoring exports over everything else, it tends to penalize all other constituent interests under its sway.

Is domestic pricing too high? Sorry – that's necessary to support the export companies. Are income gaps growing instead of shrinking? Exporters win, importers lose. Are trade barriers preventing access to the foreign goods or services you want? That's just part of favoring exports. Do currency values make everything too expensive for Japanese citizens? Sure, but that's intentional, to make the nation's goods artificially inexpensive for Japan's foreign customers.

In other words, when we in the rest of the world look at an Info-Mercantilist country such as Japan, we should not judge economic performance in the same ways we would, say, Great Britain today, or Germany, or Sweden, or the United States. And yet that is exactly what we do.

It seems, for at least the last two decades, that not a week has gone by without a headline in some major financial news medium lamenting Japan's "lost decade" (or two), how Japan is "buried in recession," and, perhaps with luck, how "Abenomics" – the economic policy of PM Shinzo Abe – or some variant (which is the same InfoMercantilist model, accelerated) will "bring Japan back."

To someone looking at Japan through the frame of its business model, none of this makes any sense. First, Japan is already doing fine; that is, its business model is doing *exactly* what it is supposed to be doing: creating the most advanced export economic machine on the planet. The function of this model is not to make everyone in Japan rich, or even well-off; the point is to make the exporters rich. What then happens to that money is a different, and itself compelling, question.

In this sense, not only has Japan succeeded, but it has likely succeeded beyond its wildest dreams. In doing so, it has redefined the model into new, more advanced versions, each an improvement over the last. In the '70s and '80s, Japanese exporters were busy putting industries invented in the U.S. out of business, including (but not limited to) manufacturers of DRAM memory chips, televisions, specialty steel, and the whole video camera / player industry. It worked: Japan got rich by exploiting these foreign inventions, and these industries were destroyed in the U.S., never to return (with the exception of a single DRAM company).

In response, the U.S. brought tariffs against Japan for "dumping," or selling copied goods at prices under their production cost. Within a very short time, Japan evolved the first major change in the business model, moving manufacturing plants (starting with cars) inside the target country's tariff borders. There was no way to tariff Hondas and Toyotas that were "Made in the USA."

Part of the reason Japan was able to sell artificially cheaply on global markets was its ongoing practice of manipulating currencies – specifically, the dollar vs. the yen. By constantly intervening, the Bank of Japan was able to "pave the way" for exporters, helping them price their products below those of their competitors. But as exporters moved more of their production operations overseas, this practice actually began to hurt sales rather than help them. Toshiba, for instance, announced recently that it was now harmed, rather than helped, when the yen was made cheaper; the company had succeeded in escaping the "gravitational pull" of mother Japan altogether.

In this way, yet another version of InfoMercantilism was born, by some measures the most advanced on the planet. If Version I was Japan-centric, and Version II involved expanded global sales, then this "Version III" of the model is defined by establishing production – and bookkeeping, banking, and even GDP – outside Japan.

While many of these trends may sound familiar to business leaders, they differ radically from their peers in most customer countries in the benefits that continue to flow from the InfoMercantilist model, such as currency manipulation, tax benefits, subsidies, preferred-purchase programs, and barriers to entry in the home market.

Toyota is a great example of this new model, with about 60% of its production now taking place on foreign shores. Who are its employees? Europeans, Americans, others – and some Japanese. Where are the cars made? In the E.U., the U.S., elsewhere – and partly in Japan. Who makes the money? Foreign subsidiaries, more than the home office. Where is it kept, and where does it show up on the accounts?

Now, *that's* a great question.

• • •

While the global press has been downplaying Japan's economic fate for decades, is it possible that the media has missed the point entirely? Is the model actually working rather than failing?

Walking down the streets of Tokyo, one does not get the feeling that anything is wrong or broken; in fact, it is quite the opposite. Tokyo, and Japan, seem to be doing just fine.

In *Stealth Japan*, financial analyst and longtime Tokyo resident Scott Foster looks deeply into all of these questions and answers them in a way that should re-establish Japan as one of the great economic success stories of our time. Or perhaps I should say, "one of the great export economic success stories."

– Mark Anderson
CEO, Strategic News Service
Friday Harbor, Washington, January 2016

# Introduction

**"ONE LAST CHANCE FOR JAPAN"**
- *Title of an article in* TIME *magazine (December 15, 2014)*

**"I don't see any reason to let people overseas know that Japan is doing just fine."**
- *Senior Japan Ministry of Economy, Trade, and Industry bureaucrat, in conversation with the author at a crowded sidewalk café in Tokyo, Summer 2012*

**"Buy my Abenomics!"**
- *Japanese Prime Minster Shinzo Abe at the New York Stock Exchange (*The Wall Street Journal, *September 27, 2013)*

This book aims to dispel the notion that Japan has become an economic irrelevance on the brink of collapse. Widely and regularly presented as news and analysis by Western journalists and financial commentators, this exaggerated and distorted picture hinders attempts to understand what is, by objective standards, a highly successful economic model that often does not fit American and European preconceptions.

The book has its origins in discussions with Mark Anderson, CEO of the Strategic News Service" (SNS) and publisher of the "SNS Global Report"; the quarterly "SNS Asia Letter," to which I have been contributing since 2006; and Mark's own writings on the subject of the Japanese economy and its frequent misrepresentation in the Western media. Anderson's concept of InfoMercantilism, which is outlined in the Foreword, serves as a baseline for the debate.

Columnist Steven Hill summed up part of the problem in a 2010 article in *The Guardian*. Unfortunately, his point of view is as relevant now as it was then:

> How, then, should we regard a country that has 5% unemployment [3.4% in December 2014], the lowest income inequality, healthcare for all its people and is one of the world's leading exporters?...
>
> Doesn't that sound like a country from which Americans and others might learn a thing or two about how to get out of the hole in which we're stuck?
>
> Not if that place is Japan. During and before the current economic crisis, few countries have been vilified as an economic basket case so much as Japan."
>
> – *Steven Hill*
> (The Guardian, *August 11, 2010*)

In late May 2012, Anderson wrote:

> This week, Nobel economist and *New York Times* columnist Paul Krugman made an interesting concession, stating that the pundits had gotten the whole story of "Japan in recession" wrong and essentially expressing the wish that the U.S. should be so lucky as to be like Japan today.
>
> One got the impression of: if Japan is in recession, I'll take two, please....
>
> One note of how poorly the global media "get," or at least report, this story:
>
> The *Wall Street Journal* ran a piece this week entitled "Cash-Rich Japanese Firms Go on Global Buying Spree."

The authors, Kana Inagaki and Atsuko Fukase, led with the line: "Flush with cash and bolstered by a strong currency, Japanese companies are in the midst of the biggest boom in overseas investment the country has ever seen."

OK, fine. Corporate Japan is minting money, and spending it on global acquisitions, right? Finally, someone gets it. But, no.

"...This boom is powered by fear, as a shrinking home market and stagnant economy threaten earnings, bankers and corporate executives say."

Keep in mind, this is on the front business page of the *WSJ* this week.

The real figures, just out, are the opposite of what was reported regarding the current status of Japanese corporate earnings this quarter: they are up an average of approximately 60%.

What?

...[Y]es, Japan's export companies are using their cash to buy major corporations all around the world. And that is the real story, for those who are paying attention to actions, not words.

*– Mark Anderson*
*("SNS Update: Asian Shifts," May 31, 2012)*

A wide range of Japanese businesses – not only exporters, but also pharmaceutical, alcoholic beverage, telecom, financial, and other companies – are buying up companies overseas. Japanese banks (and brokers, investors, politicians, golfers – pretty much anyone with money) had their fling with gross financial irresponsibility during the "bubble economy" of the late 1980s. They are in good shape now and scooping up market share dropped by their European and American competitors. Japanese exporters have also built so much production capacity offshore that it is often more accurate to refer to them as multinational manufacturers.

Something else for Americans to consider: Japan is a high-wage manufacturing economy with relatively low unemployment and no large structural trade deficit with China. So is Germany. Both countries supply China with capital goods and sophisticated manufactured products. They are facilitating China's rise from low-wage manual assembly to highly automated manufacturing, all without putting millions of their own people out of work and without undermining their own industrial bases.

With regard to Japan's overseas spending spree, Anderson has raised the possibility of corporate Japan keeping two sets of books. My research, however, indicates that for the most part (excluding financial scandals such as the Olympus incident and a few investment fiascos), the money is hidden in plain sight, in the statistics of the Ministry of Finance and the Bank of Japan, and on corporate balance sheets. But economists and Western media have tended to regard Japan's strong balance sheets as yet another sign of bad management (e.g., cash hoarding, insufficient dividend payouts, and share buybacks) rather than a logical consequence of prolonged deflation and a war chest for the purchase of technology and market share.

Contrary to much of what is published about Japan, the country has developed an economic model that does a better than average job of maintaining: a) a high level of employment, general prosperity, and social cohesion; b) competitiveness in a wide range of industries; and c) cash flow sufficient to deal with unfavorable changes in the economic environment. It is now coming to grips with a problem also faced by other advanced industrial democracies: what to do when the momentum has run out, the financial system fails, and the gains of recent decades are being lost.

"Abenomics" – the policies for economic recovery introduced by the government of Prime Minister Shinzo Abe – is often portrayed as a high-risk gamble with easy money, but is actually a practical and logical response to persistent deflation and economic stagnation. Following the victory of Abe's Liberal Democratic Party (LDP) in the elections of December 2012, the Japanese economy has started to recover, but this has been primarily due to monetary expansion and fiscal stimulus – methods used in the past to support a mercantilist, developmental economic strategy driven by exports and public-works spending. The "hard parts" – structural reform to take Japan's domestic economy beyond this model and paying down the national debt – have now begun. In the meantime, the devaluation of the yen has made it economical to build new factories in Japan. Lower prices for oil and other commodities that Japan must import are an unexpected bonus.

Despite the perennial complaints of the U.S. auto industry and the Office of the United States Trade Representative (USTR), Japan is no longer an incorrigibly protectionist society. It is particularly open to competition in cell phones, software, and other advanced technology. (Apple has nearly 50% of the Japanese cell phone market; Android phones have most of the rest.) The U.S. Congress treats it as a whipping boy. Silicon Valley views it as an opportunity. One looks backward, the other looks forward.

A victim of industrial espionage and patent infringement from South Korea and China, Japan has become a defender of intellectual property rights. Once an outsider, it is now an insider with a vested interest in the established laws and practices of the global economy. After a long period of learning – and enthusiastic teaching by the U.S. and some European nations, including (in this context) Great Britain – Japan has become an inventor of new technologies (e.g., NAND flash memory and the blue laser diode). Its economic development is inextricably interwoven with that of the West.

The travails of Sony and the rest of Japan's consumer electronics industry are not typical (any more than Motorola and Enron are typical of the U.S.). Japan remains a leading supplier of industrial robots, machine tools, power generation and other industrial equipment, engineering services, electronic components, industrial materials, and, of course, autos. It is a formidable competitor. Larger than that of Germany and more sophisticated than that of China, its economy needs to be properly evaluated.

It may help the reader to know that *Stealth Japan* is organized in this way:

Section I – "The Underestimated Economy" – reviews Abenomics, Japan's overseas investments, its demographics, and the implications of the 2020 Summer Olympics being held in Tokyo. It also notes the country's primary weaknesses, some of which are as insufficiently reported as its strengths.

Section II – "Catching Up with Europe & America" – illustrates by example the process by which industrial technology was acquired after Japan was opened to international trade by Commodore Matthew Perry of the United States Navy in the 1850s.

Section III – "From Mercantilism to Comparative Advantage" – looks into the yen / dollar exchange rate and competitive dynamics from the time of the American occupation of Japan (1945–1952) after the Asia-Pacific War to the present day.

Section IV – "From Exports to Global Production" – outlines Japan's place in the world economy and some features of its relationships with China, India, Turkey, and other countries which may not be widely known.

Section V – "Taking the InfoMercantilist Model into the Next Century" – covers some recent technological and industrial projects with long-term potential, demonstrating that despite a lagging venture capital market, Japanese innovation is alive and well, diversified, and planning for the long term.

Short essays interspersed throughout the book are presented as sidebars highlighting individual companies and technologies. These were chosen because they are complementary to the narrative and because, in the cases of Nidec, Hamamatsu Photonics, and Harmonic Drive Systems, they describe companies that have generally been ignored by Western journalists.

In addition to Mark Anderson's thinking on the subject of mercantilism, the book owes a great deal to the concept of comparative capitalism – e.g., ideas presented in *National Diversity and Global Capitalism* (eds., Suzanne Berger and Ronald Dore), Chalmers Johnson's *MITI and the Japanese Miracle*, Bob Johnstone's *We Were Burning: Japanese Entrepreneurs and the Forging of the Electronic Age*, Eamonn Fingleton's *In Praise of Hard Industries*, Andrew S. Grove's *Only the Paranoid Survive*, Richard J. Elkus' *Winner Take All: How Competitiveness Shapes the Fate of Nations*, and the writings of Clyde Prestowitz (e.g., *The Betrayal of American Prosperity: Free Market Delusions, America's Decline, and How We Must Compete in the Post-Dollar Era*).

Having worked in Japan and Korea as a securities analyst covering electronics, precision machinery, and engineering over the past 30 years, I have had the opportunity to observe the strengths and weaknesses of Japan's "hard industries" first hand.

At more than 200% of GDP, Japan has the highest national debt of any major economy – but unlike the U.S., which is in debt to the world, it owes more than 90% of that debt to itself. At U.S. $1.3 trillion, Japan also has the world's second-largest foreign exchange reserves. Cash on the balance sheets of corporate Japan amounts to nearly one-half of GDP, and large overseas investments are converting the country from an exporter to a worldwide manufacturer that makes most of its products either in the countries where they are sold or in other places, notably Southeast Asia and India, where costs are lower than they are in Japan. The numbers suggest that the Japanese economic model is more successful, and its financial situation less perilous, than is generally realized.

A word about the title: A Stealth aircraft is invisible for two reasons: superior design and obsolete radar. In the case of the Japanese economy, myopic or editorially prejudiced journalism and economic commentary are the "obsolete radar."

– Scott Foster<br>
Tokyo, January 2016

# The Underestimated Economy

"For nearly two decades, Japan has been largely irrelevant to the world economy."

– *"Japan's Revival Bid Has Global Consequences"*
(The Wall Street Journal, *July 29, 2013*)

"Japan is a disease. They're like a bug searching for a windshield. It's a dying country."

– *John Mauldin*
(*"Mauldin Economics,"* The Motley Fool, *July 22, 2010*)

For a long time now, it has been fashionable to view the Japanese economy with negativity. There are reasons for this: near-zero GDP growth, a population that has started to decline, dysfunctional politics, persistent deflation, a large and rising national debt, the hollowing-out of manufacturing (transfer of production overseas and loss of market share), and the inability of previously first-rate companies such as Sony, Panasonic, and Sharp to deal with Korean and Taiwanese competitors.

There was a joke going around London not so long ago:

**Q:** What's the definition of an optimist?

**A:** A dedicated yen equity fund manager ironing five shirts on Sunday evening.

And while the Japanese stock market was going down, the Japan

Government Bond (JGB) market was going up; it was also said that you're not an experienced investor in Japan until you've lost money shorting JGBs. Or the yen. Like the Swiss franc, the yen became a safe-haven currency, rising by about one-third against the U.S. dollar and the euro in the five years to 2012. The appreciation of the yen was a major cause of economic problems mentioned above. It also raised the question: Could Japan have been such a disaster if the currency markets liked it so much?

In the 20 years leading up to 2012 – two "lost decades," in the popular imagination – Japan's GDP amounted to $90 trillion, or $4.5 trillion per year on average. For most of that time, the country ranked second to the U.S. in economic output – until it was over-taken by China, which has more than 10x the population and 26x the land area. In 2012, Japan's GDP was a fraction less than $6 trillion, accounting for 9.6% of the world economy. This was accomplished with a high-wage, high-cost manufacturing base and accompanied by an unemployment rate lower than Germany's and one-half that of the United States.

Despite some impressive failures (e.g., Sony and Sharp), Japanese industry has been doing reasonably well, considering the limits of the domestic economy and the financial crisis of the past several years – and despite the tendency of journalists and economists to equate Chinese success with Japanese failure (an entertaining but inaccurate assessment, as we shall see).

There are many examples of Japanese corporate success:

- Japanese precision equipment and components makers provide Apple and its supply chain with machine tools, displays, batteries, memory chips, capacitors, and other components.
- Japanese companies are among Boeing's largest suppliers and its largest customers.
- Nidec and Minebea make more than 90% of the small precision motors used in hard-disk drives.

- JGC and Chiyoda have designed and built about 60% of the world's liquid natural gas (LNG) processing facilities.
- Toshiba owns Westinghouse; Softbank owns Sprint; Suntory owns Beam.

And who's driving all those cars made by Toyota, Nissan, Honda, Mazda, and Fuji Heavy Industries (Subaru)? And where are they made? For a long time now, most of Japan's industrial growth has taken place overseas, where it is excluded from Gross Domestic Product (GDP). But Western companies do not compete with Japanese GDP; they compete with Japanese companies, wherever they are.

More from the *Wall Street Journal* article excerpted at the top of this section:

> The government of Prime Minister Shinzo Abe is engaged in a high-stakes gamble to escape a cycle of paltry growth and falling prices using a combination of government spending, easy money and an ambitious overhaul of Japan's hidebound economy.
>
> If so-called Abenomics succeeds, then the world's third-biggest economy could re-emerge as a major engine of growth at a time when Europe is stagnant and China is slowing. If it fails, then Japan's Mount Fuji of government debt could come tumbling down, sending shock waves through the global economy.

In fact, Abenomics was, and still is, the only available alternative to the austerity and stagnation that caused Japan's debt problem in the first place. The greater risk is in not implementing it. The lesser risks are in managing the details. Its domestic critics have no plan of their own that can win an election.

The perception remains that Japan is weak (the terms "hidebound," "feeble," and "fossilized" are popular among Western journalists), perhaps in terminal decline, and that the Abe government's efforts to stimulate the economy are balanced on a knife edge and very high-risk – not only for Japan, but also for the world ("Abegeddon"). But even John Mauldin – writer, editor, and chairman of "Mauldin Economics" – one of Japan's harshest critics, is not entirely negative. He has called Japan a "dying country." Dying, but apparently not right away:

> There is a young gentleman in our family who has now gone to work for Sony. He sat in on the initial meeting about the home network and talked to us about where Sony (and their competitors) will be in five years. He emphasized that our wiring needs will be very different then and that we need to plan for the changes today. He and the media guy walk through the place like two kids in a candy store, talking about what can be done. So we are wiring the place for products that don't even exist yet. Somehow that appeals to the amateur futurist in me. And we will be installing more than a few Sony products, without even benefiting from the yen depreciation that I think we will see in the next several years.
>
> – John Mauldin,
> "Outside the Box" (August 20, 2013)

That's what Mauldin thinks about Sony, the last of Japan's major consumer electronics companies to seriously restructure its business.

## Abenomics

**"The combination of monetary policy, fiscal policy, and a growth strategy, I think, is exactly right. . . ."**
– Joseph Stiglitz, Professor of Economics at Columbia University
and Nobel Memorial Prize winner in Economic Sciences
(Nikkei, March 21, 2013)

"We have no choice but to accomplish economic recovery and fiscal consolidation at the same time, to maintain faith in the country and to pass on a sustainable social-security system to the next generation."

*– Japanese Prime Minister Shinzo Abe,*
*announcing his intention to raise the consumption tax*
*(Financial Times, October 1, 2013)*

"I know Japanese Prime Minister Shinzo Abe and the ruling Liberal Democratic Party are right-wing, and I'm just like any center-left person in Europe or the U.S., but I'm all for Abenomics. That is because the implicit goal of the policy mix is the welfare of the general population. I wish we had something like this in Europe."

*– Emmanuel Todd, French historian, demographer, and political*
*scientist, National Institute of Demographic Studies, Paris*
*(Nikkei, January 16, 2014)*

"Abenomics" is shorthand for a set of policies designed to reverse years of deflation and anemic economic growth. It comprises "three arrows": monetary expansion, fiscal stimulus, and structural reform. It was not presented as a policy of devaluation, but getting the yen down from levels that were pushing Japanese manufacturers to the wall has been crucial to its success. It does not include bank bailouts, because Japan's banks don't need bailing out. Nor is it a policy of austerity that punishes ordinary people for the excesses of the financial sector.

On the contrary, the aim of Abenomics is to boost growth, employment, wages, consumption, corporate profits, and tax revenues, enabling the government to start reducing the national debt. Since Prime Minister Abe took office in December 2012, progress has been made on all fronts except paying down the national debt.

In March 2013, Haruhiko Kuroda, a strong advocate of looser monetary policy, became governor of the Bank of Japan (BOJ). A former vice minister of Finance for International Affairs and president of the Asian Development Bank, Kuroda is the prime minister's partner on the monetary side of Abenomics. In his new role as governor, Mr. Kuroda immediately announced plans to double the monetary base and increase purchases of Japan Government Bonds to almost 10% of GDP in order to reach a 2% inflation target.

Some economists said this was insufficient, while others said it might cause a sharp increase in interest rates, wrecking government finances and perhaps "sending shock waves through the global economy," as the *Wall Street Journal* put it. As it turned out, the interest rate on the 10-year JGB briefly rose to 1% in May 2013 and then drifted back down to 0.6%. In mid-April 2015, it was 0.3% (while the Nikkei Stock Average was at a 15-year high). The Consumer Price Index (CPI) rose to 100 in July 2013, to 100.9 in December 2013, and to 103.7 in May 2014, after the consumption tax was raised from 5% to 8% in April. At the end of December 2014, it was 103.3.

The yen, which was already declining before Mr. Abe's election in December 2012, continued to fall. By the end of March 2014, it had dropped from a peak of JPY76/USD (in 2011) to JPY102/USD and from JPY95/EUR (in 2012) to JPY143/EUR. In addition to Mr. Kuroda's policies, this was also the result of trade and current account deficits caused by the shutdown of Japan's nuclear reactors following the disaster at Fukushima and the need to replace them with imports of fossil fuels for thermal power plants. Declines of comparable magnitude were recorded against the Chinese renminbi and South Korean won.

The depreciation of the yen resulted in increases in food, gasoline, and electricity prices far above the rate of inflation indicated by the CPI. (Sixty percent of Japan's food and all of its oil are imported.) In order to make this acceptable to the voters and prevent it from derailing economic recovery, the Abe government from the beginning promoted increases in worker compensation.

Year-end bonuses were up in 2013, salaries negotiated by unions and big business were up in Spring 2014, summer bonuses were also up, and a tightening of the labor supply caused by economic recovery put upward pressure on wages in general – a good thing, since even Uniqlo, the highly successful discount retailer of casual wear, had announced plans to raise prices.

After shrinking in Q2 and Q3 of calendar 2012, the Japanese economy expanded for six consecutive quarters (on an annualized basis, according to Ministry of Finance statistics), driven first by an increase in public-works spending (Abenomics' second "arrow") and then by exports (stimulated by the weaker yen, the first "arrow") and a broad-based recovery of corporate sales and profits. Remarkably, this was enough to create labor shortages in the construction, retail, auto, and other industries; a surge in job offers to new graduates by major companies; and, by necessity, a breakdown of those companies' reluctance to hire people who are not straight out of school.

The labor shortage has been particularly severe in the construction industry, to the extent that preparations for an easing of restrictions on the use of foreign workers are underway. Both public works and the construction of office buildings and other privately owned facilities have increased. Predictably, some foreign journalists have criticized the increase in public-works spending as a throwback to the bad old habit of Japanese politicians to build "bridges to nowhere" – but the spending is on practical and useful projects, including the post-earthquake rebuilding of Tohoku, the inspection of bridges and tunnels for earthquake damage and any necessary repairs, and the ongoing buildout of high-speed railway (Shinkansen) lines and expressways.

Incidentally, one of the least-reported stories in Japan over the past several years has been the construction of new expressways, including a ring-road system around Tokyo, which has been accompanied by the establishment of distribution centers for e-commerce and large outlet malls. This has helped reduce unemployment while

lowering prices for consumers and, in the case of the malls, creating
new suburban towns – and new opportunities to get stuck in traffic.

## Setback & Recovery

It became apparent that Abe and Kuroda had misjudged the economy's ability (or, rather, the Japanese people's willingness) to absorb
an increase in the consumption tax, which was raised from 5% to 8%
on April 1, 2014. Buying ahead of the tax increase caused annualized
GDP growth to surge to 5.8% in Q1 of calendar 2014, but this was
followed by a 6.7% decline in Q2 and a 0.5% decline in Q3. Argu-
ably, if the tax had not been raised, Abe and Kuroda would have been
seen as little more than reckless spendthrifts, and Japan would have
been severely punished by the financial markets – but in retrospect,
the increase was too large. It can be viewed as a stress-test, and the
economy failed the test.

Faced with consumer upset about an additional 3% being piled
on top of the already rising prices of necessities, and a barrage of
criticism from economists and opposition politicians question-
ing the tenets of Abenomics, the government moved quickly and
decisively. At the end of October 2014, BOJ governor Kuroda surprised the markets with another round of quantitative easing that
included raising the target for increasing the monetary base (primarily through purchases of JGBs) from ¥60 trillion – ¥70 trillion to
¥80 trillion per year (more than 15% of GDP). The stock market
jumped, supported by a nearly simultaneous announcement that
the Government Pension Investment Fund would shift its portfolio
weighting away from JGBs in favor of equities. The yen dropped from
108 to 120 to the U.S. dollar by the end of December.

On the political side, Abe shocked the nation by calling a snap
election which he pitched as a referendum on Abenomics. Defying

the opposition to present a credible alternative (which it failed to do), and promising to defer the next increase in the consumption tax from October 2015 to April 2017, his Liberal Democratic Party and coalition partner Komeito won again in a walkover, maintaining their two-thirds majority in the Lower House of the Diet and extending the time until the next mandatory election from two to four years.

Meanwhile, the price of oil has collapsed, and the prices of gas, coal, copper, and other commodities imported by Japan have also gone down. Oil industry historian and consultant Daniel Yergin calls cheaper oil Abe's "fourth arrow." It fundamentally changes the outlook for Japan's trade balance (petroleum products previously accounted for about 20% of the value of Japan's imports and oil, gas, and coal for about 33%), should lead to cheaper home heating and electricity, and has reportedly led to a rethinking of inflation targets ("BOJ Won't Act if CPI Falls on Oil Plunge," *Wall Street Journal*, February 5, 2015). It should also help support the value of the yen and, aside from inventory write-downs by importers, boost corporate profits.

The overall net profits of publicly traded companies were up 71% in the fiscal year ended March 2014. Taxes paid by these companies were up about 50%, and total corporate tax revenue for the year exceeded the government's original projection by about ¥1.5 trillion (U.S. $15 billion). It was the fourth straight year of higher corporate tax revenues, and forecasts by analysts and economists indicated that a fifth was likely to follow.

As noted by Tokyo-based investment strategist Nicholas Smith in his "Benthos" economic and stock market report, published by the broker CLSA (June 26, 2014), one-half of profit growth was accounted for by eight sectors of the economy: banks, autos, trading companies, wireless telecom, machinery, chemicals, auto parts, and pharmaceuticals. Minus electronics, this is a new profile of corporate

Japan, but certain segments of the electronics industry – components in particular – are doing very well.

GDP was up 2.2% in Q4 of 2014, and prices, as measured by the GDP deflator, were up for the first time in 17 years. Winter bonuses were also up, and average wages are likely to increase again in 2015. According to a *Nikkei* survey, hiring of university graduates is likely to rise by more than 15% in Spring 2015 to the highest level in six years.

So far, so good. That leaves the "hard parts": structural reform and paying down the national debt.

## The "Hard Parts"

Soon after taking office, Prime Minister Abe stated his intention to take Japan into the Trans-Pacific Partnership (TPP) trade negotiations, setting off a frenzy of criticism by those worried about the consequences for Japanese agriculture, healthcare, insurance, and other businesses vulnerable to free trade and deregulation. Japan joined the TPP talks in July 2013 and has been actively participating ever since.

In April 2014, with President Obama's administration unable to get (or unwilling to try to get) Fast Track negotiating authority from the U.S. Congress, Japan signed an agreement with Australia liberalizing trade in agricultural products and automobiles. By taking on Japan's entrenched farm lobby, Mr. Abe let it be known from the very start that he was serious about structural reform, and he has followed through. But that is not how it has been reported by the press or understood by investors, some of whom appear to believe that difficult political problems can be solved as quickly and easily as increasing the money supply or public-works spending.

Abenomics' "third arrow" is, in fact, a whole quiverful of arrows, including:

- Liberalization of **agriculture** (reducing rice subsidies and facilitating consolidation of small plots into economically viable units; promoting corporate farming)
- Establishment of a competitive market for **electric power** (consumers being allowed to choose suppliers; utilities likely required to spin off transmission and distribution in order to make way for new entrants; facilitation of excess power distribution between regional utilities)
- Liberalization and promotion of **medical services and technology** (deregulation of online medical product sales; clarification of standards governing medical product development and practical application of regenerative medicine; establishment of institutions equivalent to the U.S. National Institutes of Health)
- **Tax reform** (consumption tax raised from 5% to 8% in April 2014 and scheduled to rise again to 10% in April 2017; corporate tax rate to be cut from 35% (33.1% on 12/31) to less than 30%, with Germany at 29% and South Korea at 24% as useful benchmarks; reduction of subsidies for the 70% of corporations that are not currently paying tax)
- Measures to increase **women's participation in the labor force** (increasing grants for childcare and the number of daycare centers, making it easier for mothers to work and / or return to work)
- **Labor reform** (greater flexibility in hiring and firing; contracts for dispatched workers and hiring of foreign workers)
- Establishment of **special economic zones** to try out various reforms

The government is planning to establish six special economic zones, located in Tokyo (international business and innovation), Kansai (medical innovation), Fukuoka (employment system reform), Niigata (agricultural reform and large-scale farming), Yabu (agricultural reform in mountainous areas), and Okinawa (international tourism). Ideas to be tested in these zones include:

- New employment guidelines
- International medical centers employing foreign doctors and nurses
- More flexible floor space and other building and urban planning requirements
- Easier procedures for establishing agricultural corporations
- Accelerated immigration procedures and relaxation of visa requirements

Altogether, more than 35 bills related to structural reform of the economy have been passed or are being considered by the Japanese Diet, most of which seem likely to be approved by the substantial majorities in both the lower and upper houses enjoyed by Prime Minister Abe's LDP and its coalition partner, Komeito. These and other projects should keep the Japanese government busy until 2020. The question now is: will they – in combination with the efforts of the private sector – be sufficient to keep the economy growing and tax revenues rising until the national debt can be meaningfully reduced?

Paying down the national debt is the one part of Abenomics that has not yet begun. The debt has, in fact, risen since Mr. Abe took office, in part due to the increases in public-works spending aimed at stimulating growth in 2013 and offsetting the increase in the consumption tax in 2014. The other major issue for the budget is social security, which accounts for 32% of public expenditures. All additional revenues from the increase in the consumption tax will be allocated to social security.

Not surprisingly, Japanese government projections for the next few years have tax revenues rising, bond issuance declining, and the primary budget deficit (revenues before bond sales, minus expenditures before interest payments) dropping – from 6.6% of GDP in fiscal 2010 to 3.3% in fiscal 2015 and zero by 2020. Many private economists say that's not possible, but even if it is, debt-servicing is still expected to amount to 24.3% of the budget in FY 2014 (ends March 2015. Of that, bond redemption accounts for 13.7% and interest payments for 10.6%.

That leaves the Japanese economy in a "normal" – i.e., extremely challenging – situation in a world in which Europe and America have serious debt problems of their own, Europe sits on the edge of deflation, growth rates in developing countries are down, and the political situation in many parts of the world, including East Asia, is unstable. Without growth, Abenomics simply won't work, but nothing else will work, either. As for the deficit, it is the direction that matters, not the amount; and interest coverage, not the ratio of debt to GDP. Deadlines can be postponed as long as progress continues. While the LDP remains in office, a retreat into austerity is unlikely.

It should also be remembered that the primary business of Japan is business. Despite Mr. Abe's reputation as a hawk, Japanese defense spending is still only 1% of GDP (5% of the government budget). The country does not suffer from political gridlock, and Abenomics does not invite resistance by benefiting the elite at the expense of the average person.

One more very important thing: overseas investors (including Japanese investors based overseas) own less than 10% of JGBs outstanding, and the BOJ now owns about 25% – a percentage that should continue to rise, as it is now taking up about 70% of new issues. Japan also has foreign currency reserves of approximately $1.23 trillion. As things stand now, there is no way for international speculators to put an arm lock on the yen or for the International Monetary Fund (IMF) to step in and implement an austerity program.

## Ownership of Japanese Government Debt (March 2014)

( 12.3% )  ( 20.1% )

( 2.1% )

( 8.4% )

( 8.9% )

( 13.0% )

( 15.9% )

( 19.3% )

- Bank of Japan
- Insurance Companies
- Small / Medium Financial Institutions
- Domestic Banks
- Government / Public Bodies
- Overseas Investors
- Households
- Others

Source: Bank of Japan

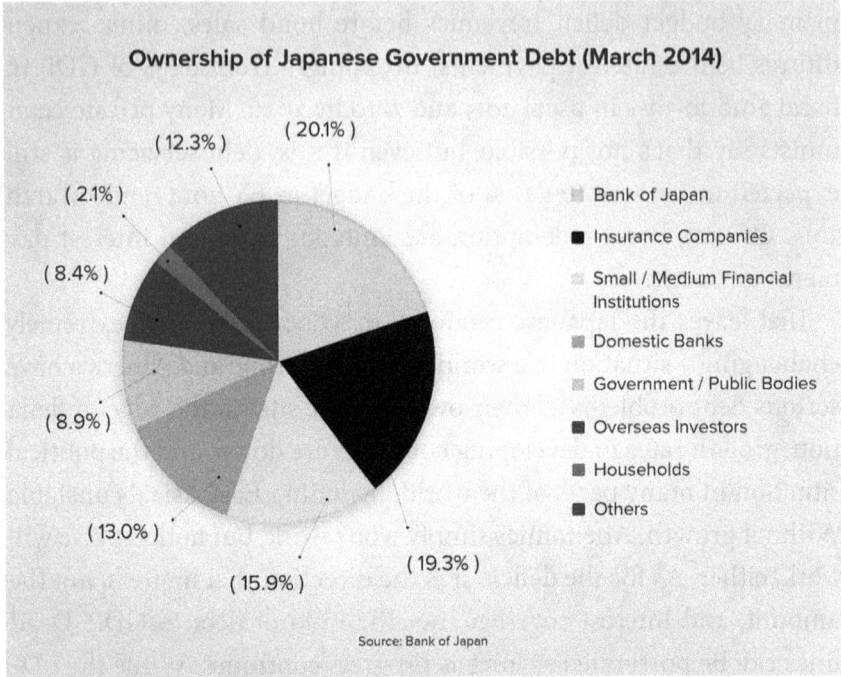

| Japan General Account Budget (Billions Yen) | | | |
|---|---|---|---|
| | FY 2013 (initial) | FY 2014 | Change |
| **Revenues** | | | |
| Tax Revenues | 43,096.0 | 50,001.0 | 6,905.0 |
| % of total | 46.5% | 52.1% | |
| Other Revenues | 4,053.5 | 4,631.3 | 577.8 |
| % of total | 4.4% | 4.8% | |
| Government Bond Issues | 42,851.0 | 41,250.0 | (1,601.0) |
| % of total | 46.3% | 43.0% | |
| Pension Related Bonds | 2,611.0 | | (2,611.0) |
| % of total | 2.8% | 0.0% | |
| Total | 92,611.5 | 95,882.3 | 3,270.8 |

| Expenditures | | | |
|---|---|---|---|
| National Debt Service | 22,241.5 | 23,270.2 | 1,028.7 |
| % of total | 24.0% | 24.3% | |
| Redemption of the National Debt | 12,338.8 | 13,138.3 | 799.5 |
| % of total | 13.3% | 13.7% | |
| Interest Payments | 9,902.7 | 10,131.9 | 229.2 |
| % of total | 10.7% | 10.6% | |
| Primary Expenditures | 70,370.0 | 72,612.1 | 2,242.1 |
| % of total | 76.0% | 75.7% | |
| Social Security | 29,122.4 | 30,517.5 | 1,395.1 |
| % of total | 31.4% | 31.8% | |
| Allocations to Local Government | 16,392.7 | 16,142.4 | (250.3) |
| % of total | 17.7% | 16.8% | |
| Public Works | 5,285.3 | 5,968.5 | 683.2 |
| % of total | 5.7% | 6.2% | |
| National Defense | 4,753.8 | 4,884.8 | 131.0 |
| % of total | 5.1% | 5.1% | |
| Total | 92,611.5 | 95,882.3 | 3,270.8 |
| | | | |
| **Japan Economic Indicators** | | | |
| | **FY 2012 (Actual)** | **FY 2013 (Est.)** | **FY 2014 (Proj.)** |
| Nominal GDP Growth | -0.2% | 2.5% | 3.3% |
| Real GDP Growth | 0.7% | 2.6% | 1.4% |
| Consumer Price Index (change) | -0.3% | 0.7% | 3.2% (1.2%*) |
| Unemployment Rate | 4.3% | 3.9% | 3.7% |
| | | | |
| *Minus 3ppt increase in the consumption tax.* | | | |

Source: Japan Ministry of Finance

## Outward-Bound Investment

> "Actually, deflation started around 1998, and it continued
> and continued until now. I mean there's been basically
> a 15 year deflation. On average, a 0.5 per cent decline in
> prices year-on-year....[that] means 0.5 per cent point
> real interest rates on cash. So corporations accumulated
> cash. They have nearly, at this stage, 50 per cent of GDP:
> in cash."
>
> – *Bank of Japan Governor Haruhiko Kuroda*
> (Financial Times *interview, January 3, 2014*)

Bank of Japan data show that total currency and deposits held by
non-financial corporations amounted to 232.4 trillion yen (U.S.
$2.3 trillion) at the end of December 2013. The figure for non-financial
companies included in the Topix 500 Index of the Tokyo Stock
Exchange – the companies that do the most prominent Mergers
and Acquisitions (M&A) deals – is much lower, but still in excess of
55 trillion yen (U.S. $550 billion) – and up about 25% in the past two
years. This, combined with limited growth prospects in the domestic market, explains why Japanese companies have been so actively
investing overseas.

Japan's cumulative outward foreign direct investment (FDI),
including M&A, has tripled over the past decade, to about U.S.
$1 trillion, or 20% of current GDP. According to RECOF Corp., an
M&A advisory, Japanese foreign acquisitions – which have been
rising since 2009 – hit a record high of 527 companies valued at
7.3 trillion yen (U.S. $73 billion) in the fiscal year ended March 14
(JIJI Press, April 6, 2014), up from 501 for 6.9 trillion yen the previous year. The most prominent acquisitions (Softbank's acquisition of
Sprint, Suntory's acquisition of Beam) and others that indicate the
breadth of activity are listed in the following table:

## Recent Japanese Outward-Bound M&A (partial list)

| Year | Acquirer | Target | Country | Value |
|---|---|---|---|---|
| **2014** | **Suntory** | **Beam** | **USA** | **$13.6 billion** |
| 2014 | Toray | Zoltek | USA | $584 million |
| 2014 | JFE Engineering | Enerkon (55%) | Indonesia | n.a. |
| 2014 | JFE Engineering | Transparent Energy Systems design division | India | n.a. |
| 2014 | Toshiba | NuGen UK (60%) | UK | GBP100m est. |
| **2013** | **Softbank** | **Sprint Nextel** | **USA** | **$21.6 billion** |
| 2013 | Softbank & Gungho | Supercell OY (51%) | Finland | $1.53 billion |
| 2013 | Suntory | Glaxo SmithKline Lucozade & Ribena | USA | $2.2 billion |
| 2013 | Torishima Pump | FEDCO (50%) | USA | n.a. |
| 2012 | Asahi Kasei | Zoll Medical | USA | $2.6 billion |
| 2013 | Dainippon Sumitomo Pharma | Boston Biomedical | USA | $2.6 billion |
| 2013 | Lixil | American Standard | USA | $342 million |
| 2013 | Otsuka Holdings | Astex Pharmaceuticals | USA | $886 million |
| **2012** | **Marubeni** | **Gavilon** | **USA** | **$5.6 billion** |
| 2012 | Marubeni | Hunt Oil Eagle Ford shale oil & gas assets (35%) | USA | $1.35 billion |
| 2012 | Hitachi | Horizon Nuclear Power | UK | n.a. |

Compiled from corporate press releases and media reports

## Recently Announced Japanese M&A Budgets

| Company | Target | Value (billion yen) | Value ($ billions) |
|---|---|---|---|
| Oji Holdings (paper) | Asia, cardboard | 150 | 1.5 |
| Nippon Paper | Biotech, electric power | 100 | 1.0 |
| Ricoh (office equipment) | Developing countries | 100 | 1.0 |
| Konica-Minolta | Medical equipment | 40 | 0.4 |
| Omron (instruments, sensors) | India, Southeast Asia | 60 | 0.6 |
| Asahi Kasei (chemicals) | Auto-related | 250 | 2.5 |
| Toray (synthetic fibers, etc.) | Advanced materials | 200 | 2.0 |
| Mitsubishi Materials | Cement, tools | 70 | 0.7 |
| IHI | Ocean development | 80 | 0.8 |
| Hitachi Zosen | Waste incineration | 40 | 0.4 |

Sources: Nikkei, company press releases

## Japan Outward Foreign Direct Investment 1996–2014 (USD billions)

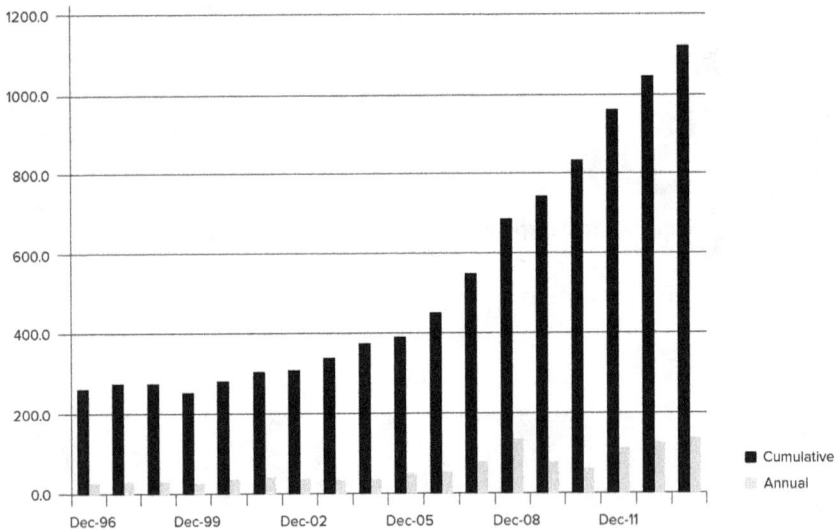

Sources: JETRO, Japan Ministry of Finance

Motor-maker Nidec (see sidebar below), Japan's M&A champion, has made 46 acquisitions since 1984, of which 15 were overseas, and 14 since the beginning of 2010 (11 overseas). These include Emerson Electric's Motors & Controls business, the Minster Machine Co., Avtron Industrial Automation, and Kinetek in the U.S.; Ansaldo Sistemi Industriali in Italy; SCD Corp. in Korea; Jiangsu Kaiyu Auto Appliance in China; and Geräte-und Pumpenbau in Germany. More are likely to follow as Nidec expands its motor and auto parts businesses around the world.

An increasing number of Japanese companies are either actively seeking M&A or considering M&A as high-speed capital spending, research and development (R&D), and a means of acquiring market access overseas. Although most of the biggest deals have been made in the United States and Europe, the largest number (roughly one-half of the total) have recently been in Southeast Asia. Companies I've interviewed also regard M&A as an efficient way to enter developing country markets in other regions. Capital spending itself has started to rise as a result of the growth created by Abenomics, and the majority of it is overseas. It would not be surprising if cumulative outward foreign direct investment rose to 30% of GDP over the next decade.

Most of the increase in outward-bound foreign direct investment, however, has been due to the relocation of manufacturing operations overseas in response to the appreciation of the yen in past years, in order to get behind actual or potential trade barriers and get closer to customers. Generally speaking, Japanese companies now seek to make products where they are sold, while maintaining "mother factories" in Japan to develop new products and manufacturing technologies. As a result, Japan has shifted from export-led growth to overseas investment-led growth.

The most striking example of this is the Japanese auto industry. In 2012, 61% of Japanese autos (unit base) were manufactured overseas; by 2017, data from industry sources indicate that this figure is likely to reach 67%, with 40% of the total manufactured in Asia.

## Japanese Auto Production by Region (2012)

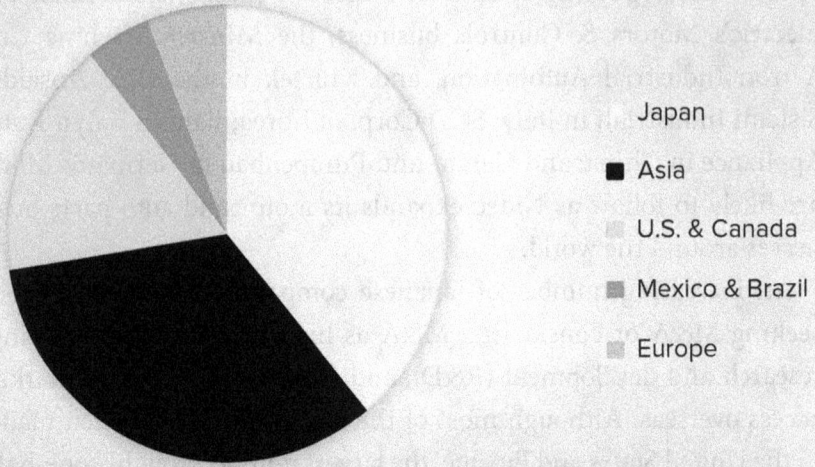

- Japan
- Asia
- U.S. & Canada
- Mexico & Brazil
- Europe

Sources: Japan Automobile Manufacturers Association, Nikkei

## Japanese Auto Production by Region (2017E)

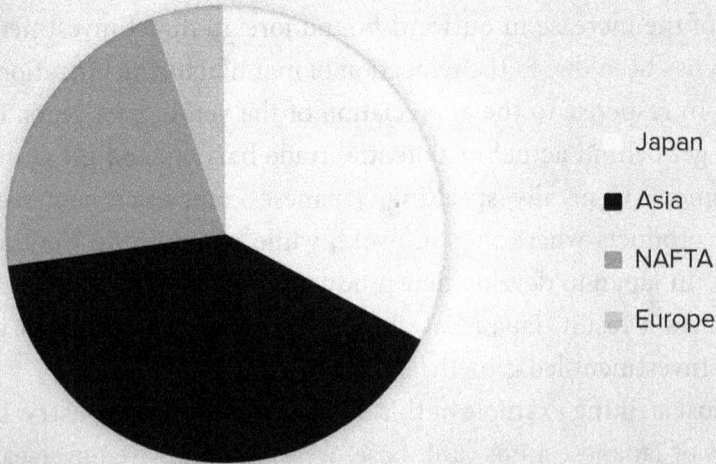

- Japan
- Asia
- NAFTA
- Europe

Sources: Japan Automobile Manufacturers Association, Nikkei

Data from Japan's top eight vehicle manufacturers (Toyota, Nissan, Honda, Suzuki, Mitsubishi, Mazda, Daihatsu, and Fuji Heavy [Subaru]) is perhaps more surprising. By May 2014, 70% of their vehicles were made and sold overseas; only 14% were exported from Japan. Following the opening of its new factory in Mexico, Honda's export ratio dropped to 1%. Nissan's was 8%, Toyota's 17%.

### Japanese Auto Production & Sales Data (May 2014)

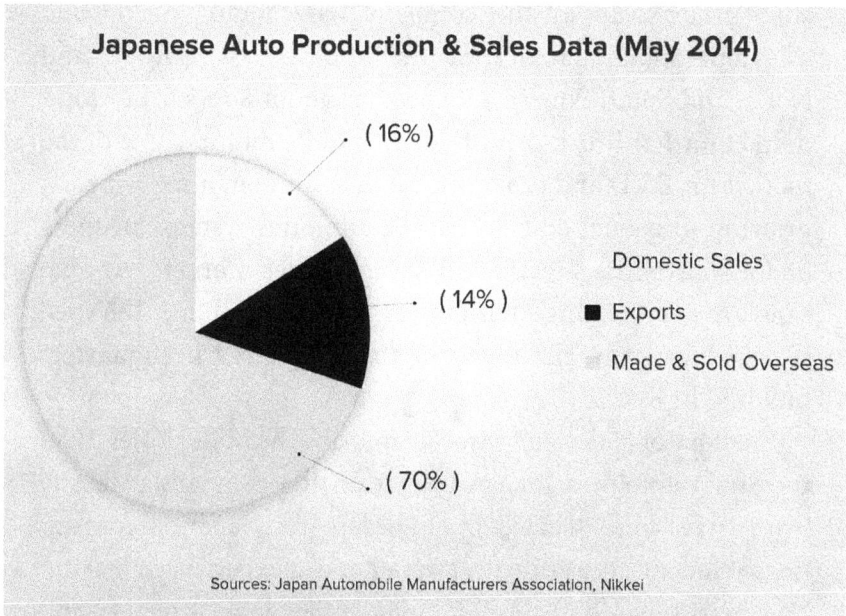

( 16% )

( 14% )

( 70% )

Domestic Sales
■ Exports
Made & Sold Overseas

Sources: Japan Automobile Manufacturers Association, Nikkei

# Nidec

Shigenobu Nagamori – founder, CEO, and chairman of Nidec Corp., the world's largest producer of brushless DC motors – has become one of Japan's most respected business managers. Mr. Nagamori and three colleagues started Nidec in a prefab shed in 1978. Today the company has manufacturing and sales operations across Asia, the Middle East, Europe, and North and South America. Nidec has about 80% of the world market for hard-disk drive (HDD) spindle motors, 60% of the market for DVD and other optical disk-drive motors, a rapidly growing auto parts and electrical automotive systems business, and a substantial presence in several other markets. Annual sales are approaching 1 trillion yen (U.S. $10 billion). The shed is now located in the lobby of the company's headquarters building in Kyoto.

The story of Nidec and Mr. Nagamori ("The Man Hotter Than the Sun") is told in manga format on the company's website (www.nidec.com). Unable to win orders from Japanese corporations reluctant to work with a small and inexperienced startup, Nagamori traveled to the U.S., "where they look at quality and not at credentials." He came back with an assignment to help 3M Corp. miniaturize cassette tape duplicators by making a smaller motor. A year later, having reduced the size of the motor by 30%, Nidec received an order for 1,000 of the new motors and started on a growth trajectory that has continued through the maturation of the PC market and the company's core HDD motor business.

In 1984, Nidec started growing through M&A, buying loss-making companies and turning them around – not by cutting staff, but by eliminating inefficiencies and motivating demoralized workers. This strategy has worked again and again – and when it hasn't worked, the company has cut its losses and looked elsewhere. The minimum target operating margin for a Nidec Group company is 10%.

So far, Nidec has acquired 46 companies in seven countries, aiming for high growth, dominant market share, and job creation. According to Mr. Nagamori, building:

> ...an organization that pays taxes and supplies useful goods to society is a positive goal, but of primary importance is to provide a place where many, many people can work safely and securely. The creation of employment is the largest contribution to society.
> – *"Nidec's Nagamori Gets Hands Dirty"*
> (The Wall Street Journal, *August 18, 2010*)

Nidec benchmarks against Emerson, Softbank, and Fast Retailing (Uniqlo) – Emerson because of its dynamic management and high profit margins, Softbank and Fast Retailing because they were also built and are run by single-minded entrepreneurs like Mr. Nagamori. In contrast to Toyota, there is no attempt to teach the world at large the Nidec Way. The best, and perhaps only, way to learn how Nidec does things is to be taken over by Nidec.

Nidec is included in the JPX-Nikkei Index 400, a stock market index made up of investor-friendly companies that make efficient use of capital. The creation of this index in 2013 was seen as a tool to raise standards of corporate governance in Japan. Criteria for selection include operating profit, return on equity, dividend payout, and the presence of outside directors (a relatively new phenomenon in Japan).

## Nidec M&A History

| Year | In Japan | Overseas | Country |
|------|----------|----------|---------|
| 1984 | | Trin Corp. axial fan division | USA |
| 1989 | DC Pack | | |
| 1989 | Shinano Tokkio | | |
| 1991 | | Power General Corp. | USA |
| 1992 | Japan Seagate precision composite parts division | | |
| 1993 | Masaka Electronics | | |
| 1995 | Kyoritsu Machinery | | |
| 1995 | Shimpo Industries | | |
| 1996 | Daisan Industry | | |
| 1997 | Tosok | | |
| 1997 | Read Electronics | | |
| 1997 | Kyori Kogyo | | |
| 1997 | Nidec Power General | | |
| 1998 | | Cone Art Kilms Corp. | Canada |
| 1998 | Copal | | |
| 1998 | Copal Electronics | | |
| 1998 | PST | | |
| 1998 | Shibaura Nidec | | |
| 1999 | Kyowa Hightech | | |
| 1999 | Nemicon | | |
| 2000 | Y-E Drive | | |
| 2000 | | Seagate motor division of Rangsit Plant | Thailand |
| 2003 | Sankyo Seiki | | |
| 2006 | FUJISOKU | | |
| 2007 | Japan Servo | | |

| 2010 | | ACC Corp. home appliance motor division | Italy |
|------|--|------|------|
| 2010 | | SC Wado Component Co. | Thailand |
| 2010 | | Emerson Electric motors & controls business | USA |
| 2011 | Sanyo Seimitsu | | |
| 2012 | | The Munster Machine Co. | USA |
| 2012 | | Ansaldo Sistemi Industriali | Italy |
| 2012 | | Avtron Industrial Automation | USA |
| 2012 | | SCD Corp. | South Korea |
| 2012 | | Kinetek Group Inc. | USA |
| 2012 | | Jiangsu Kaiyu Auto Appliance | China |
| 2014 | Mitsubishi Materials C.M.I. | | |
| 2014 | Honda Elesys | | |
| 2015 | | Geräte-und Pumpenbau | Germany |
| 2015E | | China Tex SR motor assets | China |

Source: Nidec [E: Announced in December 2014]

# Running Out of People?

Japan has a population of about 127 million living in a land area of 378 square kilometers. By comparison, California has a population of about 40 million in an area of 424 square kilometers. Much of California consists of sparsely populated desert and mountains. Much of Japan consists of forested, but steep and sparsely populated, mountains. Lowland Japan is crowded with cities and farms, with a population density characteristic of Asian rice producers.

Since the first census taken by the new Meiji government in 1872, Japan's population has increased by 3.7x, but the growth has now stopped, and decline has begun. The number of Japanese between the ages of 15 and 64 – often taken as a proxy for the working population – peaked at 87 million in the mid-1990s. By 2013, it was down to 79 million, or 62% of the total. People 65 or older made up 25% of the total. Children up to the age of 14 accounted for 13%. Total population peaked at 128 million in 2008. Japan's fertility rate is 1.4 – up from a record low of 1.26 in 2005. It was last above 2.0 in 1974. Demographers estimate that Japan's total population will decline to 87 million by 2060 if the fertility rate – or the nation's immigration policy – doesn't change.

## Japan: Total Population (in millions)

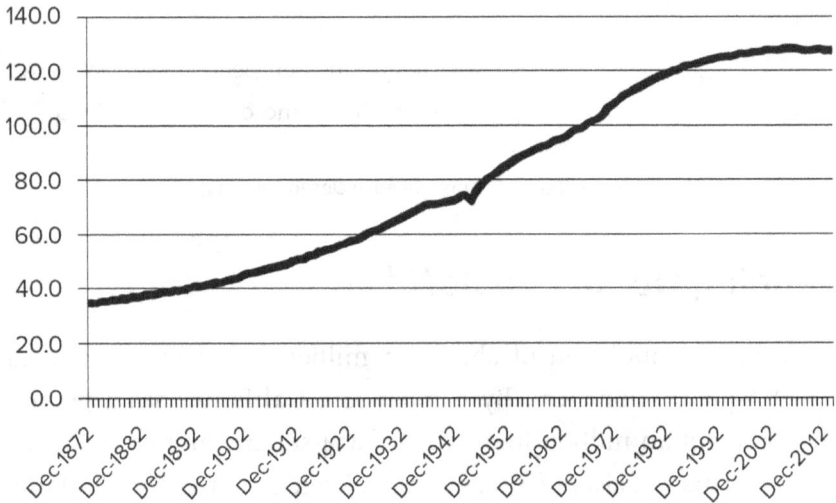

Sources: Statistics Bureau, Ministry of Internal Affairs and Communications

## Population of Japan by Age Group (in millions)

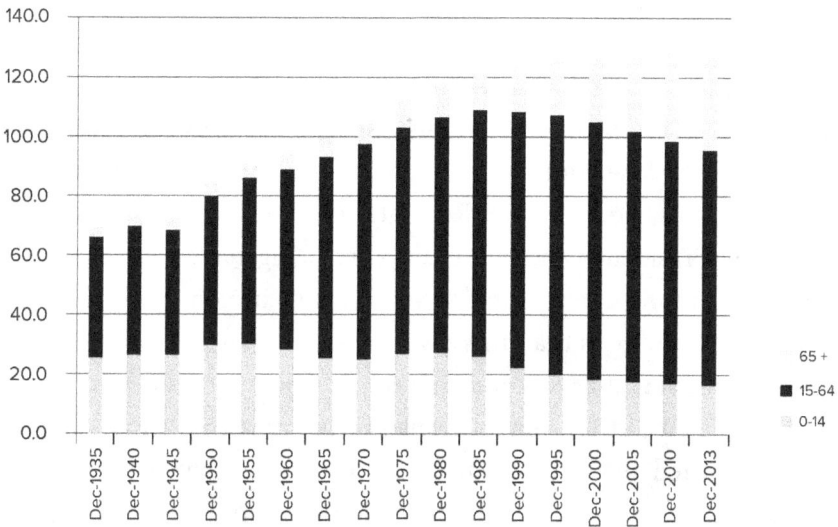

Sources: Statistics Bureau, Ministry of Internal Affairs and Communications

In May 2014, a government panel headed by the chairman of the Japan Chamber of Commerce and including the minister for Economic and Fiscal Policy set a goal of maintaining a population of at least 100 million over the next 50 years. In order to do that, the panel concluded, the fertility rate needs to rise to 2.07 by 2030. That translates into supporting an increase in the number of children per married couple from 1.7 to 2.4 – through tax incentives, child support, and other measures. The chairman emphasized that everyone in Japan should "share our sense of crisis that an extremely difficult future lies ahead if the situation is left as it is" (*Nikkei*, May 14, 2014).

On the subject of immigration, the panel's report stated that "the effects need to be considered in a comprehensive manner" (*ibid.*). The independent Japan Center for Economic Research has proposed increasing the number of foreign residents in Japan by 200,000 per year, which would raise the share of immigrants in the population from less than 2% today to 6% by 2050. This would make it much easier to keep the population above 100 million, but at present it is a politically unacceptable solution.

As in many other countries, immigration reform and the import of foreign workers are contentious issues, but a growing sense that Japan is too closed for its own good and practical necessity are driving step-by-step change. Regulations regarding the granting of permanent residence and citizenship are being eased, and there are noticeably more foreign employees working in convenience stores, restaurants, and bars than there were a few years ago.

In April 2014, at a joint meeting of the Council on Economic and Fiscal Policy and the Competitiveness Commission, Prime Minister Abe supported the establishment of procedures that would enable businesses in Japan to hire more foreign workers. There are already serious labor shortages in the fields of healthcare and construction, and the latter is expected to get worse as Tokyo prepares for the 2020 Summer Olympics.

There is an inherent contradiction between the large-scale importation of low-cost labor and the need to support consumer spending, tax revenues, and larger families by raising wages. Public-opinion polls and other sources, including an internal survey by construction equipment maker Komatsu, indicate that the Japanese would like to have more children but can't afford to, particularly in Tokyo, Osaka, and other big cities. The challenge for the government is to keep the labor supply at levels that support rising incomes on the one hand and prevent bottlenecks on the other.

On a 50-year view, this looks like a daunting task. On a 5- to 10-year view, it looks manageable. Ten years from now, the social context in which immigration is discussed is likely to be very different, and proposals such as that of the Japan Center for Economic Research may not seem at all radical.

Two important social trends should also make it easier for Japan to deal with an aging and declining population. Unlike in France, where the response to economic difficulties has been to cut working hours and lower the retirement age, most older Japanese people prefer to (and, in many cases, have to) keep working. Rather than retire their most experienced employees, Japanese corporations are making arrangements to extend their working lives, either on their own initiative or as required by new government regulations.

For most of the postwar period, the official retirement age was 55. The new standard, which is being adopted by more and more companies, is 65. Including jobs found after retirement, the average Japanese now works until almost the age of 70, and the number of people over 70 who are still working is rising. The country is full of "silver centers" that dispatch elderly workers to part-time jobs.

The number of women returning to work after child rearing is also increasing, helped by more favorable attitudes in business and local government, and the Abe administration is planning to expand the availability of daycare services for working mothers. Bringing more women into the workforce and increasing their presence in managerial positions without putting downward pressure on the birth rate is one of Prime Minister Abe's major policies. As the number of working mothers and the retirement age rise, the worker / dependent ratio should improve, taking pressure off the national budget.

Finally, the labor force available to Japanese corporations worldwide is effectively unlimited, and, as their growth opportunities are now primarily overseas, this workforce is increasingly being utilized. This is true of the Japanese auto, electronics, machinery, and other manufacturing industries, and some non-manufacturing businesses as well.

The example of Yokogawa Electric illustrates this point. Yokogawa makes control systems and equipment for the oil and gas, petrochemical, and other processing industries. In this business, it competes with ABB, Siemens, Honeywell, Emerson, Invensys, and others, ranking fourth after Honeywell in worldwide market share. At the end of March 2004, Yokogawa had 17,300 employees, of which 6,100 were overseas and 11,200 were in Japan. Ten years later, at the end of March 2014, it had 19,800 employees, of which 11,400 were overseas and 8,400 in Japan. By March 2019, management expects overseas employees to account for 70% of the company's workforce. About 5% of the total will be in the U.S., with cheaper engineers in Singapore and India backing them up.

## The 2020 Olympics & the 2021 Problem

The role of what economist John Maynard Keynes called "animal spirits" in Japan's economic recovery cannot be overestimated. By the time Shinzo Abe and the LDP launched their campaign to "Restore Japan" in the second half of 2012, the nation had been utterly demoralized by incompetent government, economic malaise, and non-stop commentary from economists, journalists, and academics emphasizing that the decline was probably terminal. The demographic problem looked so intractable that some even said that the Japanese people might disappear. On top of that came the Tohoku earthquake and tsunami, and the nuclear disaster at Fukushima, and the flooding in Thailand, which caused major damage to Japanese industry.

Following Junichiro Koizumi's resignation in September 2006, Japan had six prime ministers in six years (Mr. Abe himself was the first). In 2009, Yukio Hatoyama's Democratic Party of Japan crushed the LDP, promising an end to corruption and incompetence, then took both to new levels. Policymaking was confused, relief funds for Tohoku were redirected to the whaling industry, and the economy remained weak.

The LDP spent its time in the wilderness plotting its comeback and devising a plan to get the country back in gear. Its victory in December 2012 was also overwhelming. The corrupt and aging LDP that voters threw out in 2009 had remade itself into a practical and generally younger agent for change. Mr. Abe combines an energetic and usually cheerful demeanor with straight talking, backbone, and long-term plans. Three months after his election, he told the Industrial Competitiveness Council: "I want to position the next five years as an emergency structural reform period" (*Nikkei*, March 15, 2013). Following his reelection in December 2014, he should remain in office for at least that long.

Peter Tasker, one of the most astute analysts of Japan, describes the situation this way:

> Ultimately, Abenomics is a delicate experiment in psychological alchemy.... The key is ki.... 'Keiki,' the Japanese word for economic conditions, contains the character 'ki,' meaning 'spirit.' Keynes also emphasized the importance of 'animal spirits....'
>
> In recent years, there have been signs of positive incremental changes that tended to be ignored until the arrival of Abenomics. The most important has been corporate profitability, which has managed an impressive rise since the turn of the century, despite the headwinds of a strong currency and weak domestic demand. At the top of the cycle in 1999/2000, the Topix index [Tokyo Stock Price Index] generated earnings per share of a mere 25 yen. This year over 80 yen is expected.
>
> – *"Austin Powers on Abenomics"*
> (*www.petertasker.asia*, August 21, 2013)

In September 2013, the International Olympic Committee chose Tokyo as the site of the 2020 Summer Olympic Games. Prime Minister Abe, who had campaigned hard for the Games, flew to Buenos Aires for the balloting. Tokyo's victory over Istanbul and Madrid gave the Japanese an exciting and challenging long-term project which overlaps with and contributes to Abenomics.

Books of maps and commentary on the building of new infra-structure and the beautification of Tokyo for the Games have been published. A new downtown promenade called MacArthur Road that Tokyo Governor Masuzoe Yoichi hopes will be Tokyo's Champs Élysées has been opened. While preparing for the Games, Governor Masuzoe and other government officials, following the example of London, are trying to work them into long-term development plans for the city. The goal is to leave a positive legacy rather than a finan-cial hangover and to avoid a post-Games slump – the 2021 Problem. That is the time frame within which Japanese economic and social policy is now being developed.

## Inherent Weaknesses

While Japan is now doing reasonably well, the country has weak-nesses that could undermine Prime Minister Abe's attempts to create a sustainable economic recovery and limit its competitiveness over the longer term. These include:

1.  **Over-reliance on hardware.** Dedicated to making things, the Japanese were slow to grasp the concept of outsourcing semi-conductor production to foundries such as TSMC and slow to appreciate the significance of the Internet, software (except game software), and the combination of hardware, software, and Web-based applications created by Apple, big data, and even 3D printing. They may not win the battle to develop next-generation manufacturing based on software, big data, and robotics.

2.  **Homogeneity.** Both a strength and a weakness, the extreme homogeneity of Japanese society makes it unlikely that Japan

will create "the next Google" – a goal often mentioned in discussions on how to promote venture businesses in Japan. It is much easier for a Japanese scientist or engineer to succeed at an American or other Western university or company than it is for a foreigner to succeed in Japan.

3. **A high level of dependency on the outside world.** Japan cannot maintain an advanced industrial economy without access to overseas markets and natural resources. It is vulnerable to foreign economic and political developments that it cannot control, and to Korean and Chinese hostility, which it has done much to provoke.

4. **A shortage of independent capital and an aversion to risk.** Depending on the estimate, America has at least 20 times more venture capital than Japan, and many times more entrepreneurs and startups. Citing himself as an example, Prime Minister Abe is promoting the idea that people who have failed should be allowed to try again, but it is an uphill battle against entrenched attitudes.

5. **A preference for hard money and austerity among the bureaucrats at the Ministry of Finance.** If the economy falters or the government fails to reduce the deficit, fiscal conservatives could regain the initiative, raise taxes, cut spending, and take the country back into the stagnation from which it has just emerged.

## II.

# Catching Up with Europe and America

Japan's drive to acquire Western technology was originally inspired by European and American imperialism; practical interest in weaponry, manufacturing, and medicine, and scientific curiosity. It dates back to the 1543 arrival of Portuguese explorers in Japan, which was quickly followed by Japanese manufacture and technical improvement of European-style guns, as well as the study of European science and technology via the Dutch trading post established on the island of Dejima in Nagasaki harbor in 1609.

The first Englishman known to have reached Japan was William Adams, who arrived on a Dutch vessel in 1600. Adams became an advisor to the shogun Tokugawa Ieyasu and supervised the construction of Japan's first European-style ship. His story is told in the 1975 novel *Shogun* by James Clavell.

The adoption of Western knowledge slowed to a crawl in the 1630s, when, in a successful effort to stop the advance of Christianity and colonialism, foreign travel was made a capital offense and trade was severely restricted. It did not re-accelerate until Western navies, strengthened by more than two centuries of technological progress, arrived in the mid-19th century.

Since then, Japan has developed a breadth and depth of technological sophistication unmatched outside Western Europe and the United States. This has been accomplished through long and involved cooperation with Great Britain, the United States, Germany, and other European countries; respect for learning and reverence for teachers; and a strong drive for self-sufficiency.

## Commodore Perry's Toy Train

When Commodore Mathew C. Perry of the United States Navy and his squadrons arrived in Tokyo Bay in 1853, and again in 1854, to open Japan to international commerce, they brought presents. One of those presents was a working model of a steam railway, which was subsequently set up on the beach. The railway was very popular with Japan's military nobility – the samurai – and led to an enthusiasm for trains that is probably unmatched anywhere in the world.

After the Meiji Restoration in 1868, which replaced the shogunate with a modernizing government, Sir Harry Smith Parkes, British consul-general in Japan, recommended the rapid construction of railways to senior Japanese officials. Locomotives and passenger cars arrived from Great Britain in 1871, and service began on a line running between Tokyo and Yokohama the following year.

By 1889, railways had been built on all four of Japan's main islands. The Japanese produced their first steam locomotive in 1893 and built their first electric railway in 1895. By 1906, 11 years later, they were operating railways in Taiwan, Korea, Karafuto (Sakhalin), and Manchuria (the South Manchurian Railway, built by the Russians but taken over by the Japanese after their victory in the Russo-Japanese War). The first Japanese railways were financed through bonds issued in London.

An engineer training college, headed by an Englishman, was established at Osaka Station in 1877. Nearly 300 British and other foreign railway specialists were hired to design, build, operate, and maintain Japan's new railways – and to teach the Japanese how to do their jobs. By 1905, less than 30 years later, they were gone. By 1920, the quality of Japanese steel and workmanship was good enough that all the materials and parts required to build a railway could be sourced in Japan. By 1940, Japanese government railway lines extended for 18,400km (11,433 miles) and private railway lines for another 8,900km (5,530 miles), in a country smaller than the state of California.

The Shinkansen (or "New Trunk Line" – known as the "Bullet Train" in English) was originally proposed in 1939 as a faster and higher-capacity method of transport from Tokyo to the port city of Shimonoseki at the southwestern end of the island of Honshu, opposite Korea and Japan's Asian empire. There were plans to extend the line through a tunnel to Korea and on to Beijing, but construction was suspended during the Pacific War and not restarted until 1959. The first section of the line – the Tokaido Shinkansen running from Tokyo to Osaka – was opened in 1964, just in time for the Tokyo Summer Olympics.

At present, the Shinkansen network extends for more than 2,500km (1,553 miles), from northern Honshu to southern Kyushu, with extensions to the northern island of Hokkaido and the city of Kanazawa on the Japan Sea under construction. Operating at speeds up to 320km per hour, with up to 11 trains per hour between Tokyo and Osaka at peak hours, it carries more than 150 million passengers per year.

Railway equipment and systems are a big business for Japan's large heavy-electrical and machinery conglomerates and numerous smaller companies specializing in railway cars, signaling, and other equipment, with markets in Japan, Asia, North America, and Europe.

In 2012, in the first round of the U.K.'s Intercity Express upgrade program, Hitachi beat out local competition to win a £2.4 billion order for electric trains and long-term maintenance. The U.K. government aims to improve the nation's infrastructure and help rebuild its manufacturing base and engineering supply chain by creating a technologically advanced railway system, and Hitachi hopes to use its success in the U.K. as a springboard to continental Europe and other markets. To this end, Hitachi has moved the headquarters of its global railway business to the U.K.

In July 2013, Hitachi Rail Europe received a £1.2 billion follow-on order for 30 nine-car high-speed electric trains to run on the East Coast Main Line from London to Aberdeen. The contract includes nearly three decades of maintenance, and the cars will be built at Hitachi's Newton Aycliffe factory in northeast England.

The Japanese are also having a major influence on new passenger railway standards in the U.S. Railway-technology.com reports that the proposed California High-Speed Rail network "will reflect the design of the new Series 500 and 700 Shinkansen trains that operate… in Japan and French TGV (*Train à Grande Vitesse*)."

The introduction of maglev (magnetic levitation) trains is expected to reduce travel time from Tokyo to Nagoya from about two hours on today's Shinkansen to 40 minutes; and by 2045 to Osaka – which currently takes about three hours – to 67 minutes. JR Tokai hopes to export its maglev technology to the U.S. for use between Washington, DC, and Boston. Commercial service on the Tokyo-Nagoya section of the Linear Chuo Shinkansen is scheduled to start in 2027, with partial local services commencing in time for the 2020 Tokyo Olympics.

## A Memorial to Thomas Edison

Iwashimizu Hachimangu is an ancient Shinto shrine located on the peak of Otokoyama in the city of Yawata, halfway between Kyoto and Osaka. It was founded in the year 859 to watch over Kyoto and the Imperial Household and has remained one of the most important shrines in Japan ever since. To get there, take the Keihan Electric Railway Line to Yawata-shi station, then either ride the cable car or walk to the top the mountain. Otokoyama is an island of green in a sea of low-rise concrete buildings, roads, and railway lines. The forest in which the shrine is located is thick with cedar and bamboo. In a plaza near the shrine stand memorials to the musician and composer Nakao Tozan, the Boy Scouts, and Thomas Edison.

In his laboratory in Menlo Park, New Jersey, in 1879, Edison produced his first electric light bulb, using a carbonized cotton filament. It lasted 45 hours before burning out. Working on the assumption that a light bulb would need to last at least 600 hours in order to be commercially viable, he began to test other potential filament materials. Finding a bamboo fan in his laboratory, he tested its fibers and found that a filament made from that particular bamboo lasted about 200 hours. He then dispatched several of his assistants abroad in search of the bamboo best suited to serve as filament for electric light bulbs.

The following year, one of those assistants, William H. Moore, went to Tokyo, where he met with Prime Minister Ito Hirobumi and War Minister Yamagata Aritomo. They advised Moore to go to Kyoto.

In Kyoto, the governor of Kyoto Prefecture suggested that Moore try the bamboos of Sagano and Yawata. The *madake* bamboo of Yawata won the filament contest, lasting 2,450 hours. Thereafter, Yawata bamboo was used in light bulbs manufactured by Edison companies (including Edison General Electric) until 1894, when it was replaced with filaments made from other sources of cellulose.

In 1929, the Japanese government celebrated the 50th anniversary of Edison's first light bulb with the establishment of an Edison memorial in Yawata. It was rebuilt on the present site in 1980. Today, visitors to Iwashimizu Hachimangu can buy a five-sided wooden prayer tablet (*ema*) with Edison's picture on the front and "1% inspiration, 99% perspiration" written on the back in Japanese. By coincidence, February 11 is both Japan's National Foundation Day and Edison's birthday. Both are celebrated at the Iwashimizu Hachimangu shrine.

Several Japanese researchers visited and worked for Edison in the United States. Among them were Kunihiko Iwadare, who went on to found the Nippon Electric Company (NEC), and Ichisuke Fujioka, who in 1890 founded the company that eventually became Toshiba. When Fujioka told Edison that he intended to establish an electric power industry in Japan, Edison is said to have replied:

> Bringing electricity to Japan is a noble ambition. But no matter how much electric power a country may have at its disposal, it's doomed if it has to import electrical appliances. So start with manufacturing electrical appliances. Make Japan self-sufficient as a nation.
>
> – *Ichisuke Fujioka Biography,*
> *Biografi Tokoh (Indonesia)*

Even if Edison did not actually speak these words, they are what the Japanese wanted to hear.

## The Origins of Toshiba

In 1873, William Edward Ayrton, an English physicist and electrical engineer serving with the Indian Government Telegraph, accepted an invitation from the Japanese government to become Chair of Natural Philosophy and Telegraphy at the Imperial College of Engineering in Tokyo. Ichisuke Fujioka was one of his students. In addition to teaching the fundamentals of the telegraph, electric arc light, and other leading-edge technologies of the time, Professor Ayrton advised his students to "respect fundamental principles; constantly challenge yourself; don't just imitate – make something even better."

Fujioka graduated at the head of his class and began a career as a teacher. It was 1884 when he visited Edison's Menlo Park laboratory. Returning home, he advised the government and industry to introduce the electric light bulb to Japan. Two years later, he resigned his post at the university in order to work on the development of light bulbs and other projects. In 1890, he established Hakunetsu-sha Co. Ltd. (*hakunetsu* means "white-hot," or "incandescent") to manufacture light bulbs on a commercial basis.

Fujioka also designed Japan's first electric passenger train and the motor that drove it, supervised the construction of the Kyoto Electric Railway – Japan's first electric railway, which began service in 1895, and was involved with the design and construction of several power stations. In 1905, facing severe financial difficulties, Fujioka's company changed its name to Tokyo Electric and formed a joint venture with General Electric, which provided more advanced light bulb–making technology and acquired 51% of the company's shares.

In 1873, the Japanese government commissioned another company, Tanaka Engineering Works, to develop telegraphic equipment. It went bankrupt 20 years later and was taken over by Mitsui Bank, which renamed it Shibaura Engineering Works. In 1910, this company also formed a joint venture with General Electric. In 1939, the two companies merged to form Tokyo Shibaura Electric Co. The relationship with General Electric, which had been severed during the war, was reestablished in 1953, with GE owning 24% of shares. In 1984, the company's name was shortened to Toshiba. GE is no longer a major shareholder, but the two companies have cooperated in gas turbine combined-cycle power generation projects since 1982.

The advice of Thomas Edison and William Ayrton and the work of Ichisuke Fujioka are reflected in Toshiba's current product line-up, which includes electric home appliances, lighting, a wide range of power generation equipment, and railway transportation equipment and systems. Toshiba is a leading producer of LED light bulbs, steam turbines, nuclear power plants (it owns Westinghouse), geothermal power plants, NAND flash semiconductor memory chips (invented by Fujio Matsuoka while working at Toshiba), power semiconductors,

POS systems, and medical equipment. It also has a substantial presence in the markets for flat-panel TVs, data storage devices, solar power systems, and numerous other electrical and industrial products.

Toshiba employs more than 110,000 people in Japan and more than 200,000 worldwide, with annual sales exceeding ¥6 trillion (USD $50 billion). All of this evolved from the study of British and American technology, but the student has now joined the faculty.

## The Evolution of NEC

A graduate of Japan's Imperial College of Engineering, Kunihiko Iwadare traveled to the United States in 1886 and went to work for… Thomas Edison. In 1887, he returned to Japan and joined the Osaka Electric Lamp Co. Eight years later, he started his own business as a sales agent for General Electric and Western Electric. In 1898, he formed a limited partnership with Western Electric to market telephone equipment in Japan. The following year, the partnership was converted into a joint stock company called Nippon Electric Co., which was 54% owned by Western Electric. This was Japan's first international joint venture.

Nippon Electric Co. (renamed NEC Corp. in 1983) grew with the Japanese economy, becoming one of the world's leading makers of telecommunications equipment in the process. It began research into transistors and computers in the 1950s, started to develop ICs in 1960, launched its Zero Defect campaign in 1965, and entered the markets for mainframe computers and PCs in the 1970s and 1980s.

In the mid-1980s, low prices and high quality made it possible for NEC and other Japanese semiconductor makers to drive Intel out of the DRAM market. On this subject, then-Intel CEO Andy Grove wrote: "…[T]he quality levels attributed to Japanese memories [by Hewlett-Packard] were beyond what we thought were possible" (*Only the Paranoid Survive*; Crown Business, 1999). Intel subsequently abandoned the DRAM market and shifted its focus to microprocessors.

In 1985, Intel, National Semiconductor, and Advanced Micro Devices filed a petition with the Department of Commerce alleging Japanese dumping of EPROM, and Micron Technology filed a petition alleging Japanese dumping of DRAM. These actions led to the imposition of anti-dumping duties and the U.S.–Japan Semiconductor Trade Agreement of 1986, which targeted a 20% share of the Japanese semiconductor market for American companies. That target was never reached, and by the early 1990s, NEC was the world's largest maker of semiconductors. Its fortunes peaked with sales of more than JP¥5 trillion and more than 150,000 employees around the world.

After that, things went rapidly downhill as management failed to respond effectively to competition from the U.S., Korea, and Taiwan. The semiconductor business was eventually abandoned. The PC business remained trapped in the domestic market, which was no longer growing, and was finally transferred to a joint venture 51%-owned by Lenovo in 2011. The telecommunications business was overwhelmed, first by the Internet revolution in the U.S. and then by rapidly growing competition from China. At present, due to a combination of defeat, retreat, and restructuring, sales are down to about JP¥3 trillion and the company has about 110,000 employees.

But NEC never lost the innovative spirit imparted by Edison. In 1991, Sumio Iijima, a physicist working for the company, made what became the most widely publicized discovery of carbon nanotubes. (Others had observed them much earlier, beginning with the Russian scientists L.V. Radushkevich and V.M. Lukyanovich, who published their findings in the Soviet *Journal of Physical Chemistry* in 1952.) At the turn of the century, NEC built the Earth Simulator (ES) supercomputer to run climate models and conduct other projects for the Japan Aerospace Exploration Agency (JAXA), the Japan Atomic

Energy Research Institute, and the Japan Marine Science and Technology Center. From 2002 to 2004, ES was the fastest supercomputer in the world.

NEC was also a key developer and supplier of the ion engines, computer and communications systems, cameras, distance sensors, and electronic components for JAXA's *Hayabusa* (Peregrine Falcon) asteroid probe. Launched from Japan's Uchinoura space center in May 2003, *Hayabusa* became the first spacecraft to land on an asteroid – touching down on a small (535m x 294m x 209m) rock named *25143 Itokawa* (after Hideo Itokawa, one of the pioneers of Japanese rocketry) and taking samples in November 2005, returning to Earth in June 2010. *Hayabusa* was the first space probe to be powered by ion engines. A few days after *Hayabusa*'s return, NEC signed an agreement with Aerojet (now Aerojet Rocketdyne) to supply ion propulsion systems to the U.S. and Japanese aerospace markets. Like Toshiba, it is now a well-established contributor to advanced technology.

## Japanese Nobel Prize Winners

While the histories of Toshiba, NEC, and other Japanese companies illustrate the process by which European and American science and technology was assimilated, the Nobel Prize is a measure of the degree to which that process has succeeded. So far, there have been 22 Japanese Nobel laureates – nowhere near the top of the list, but the highest number for any non-European or non-U.S. nationality. Ten of the prizes have been in Physics, seven in Chemistry, two in Physiology or Medicine, two in Literature, and one Nobel Peace Prize.

Aside from Kenzaburo Oe's and Yasunari Kawabata's prizes in Literature, the most prominent have been the Physics awards. In 1965, Sin-Itiro (Shinichiro) Tomonaga shared the prize with Julian Schwinger and Richard Feynman for their "fundamental work in quantum electrodynamics, with deep-ploughing consequences for the physics of elementary particles." In 1973, Leo Esaki shared the prize in Physics with Ivar Giaever and Brian David Josephson for their "experimental discoveries regarding tunneling phenomena in semiconductors and superconductors, respectively." The most recent Physics prizes won by Japanese scientists are the subject of the next section.

## Japanese Nobel Laureates

| Year | Laureate | Prize |
|------|----------|-------|
| 2014 | Shuji Nakamura | Physics |
|      | Isamu Akasaki |  |
|      | Hiroshi Amano |  |

"For the invention of efficient blue light-emitting diodes which has enabled bright and energy-saving white light sources."

| 2012 | Shinya Yamanaka | Physiology or Medicine |
|------|-----------------|------------------------|

"For the discovery that mature cells can be reprogrammed to become pluripotent" – shared with John B. Gurdon.

| 2010 | Akira Suzuki | Chemistry |
|------|--------------|-----------|
|      | Ei-ichi Negishi |  |

"For palladium-catalyzed cross couplings in organic synthesis" – shared with Richard F. Heck.

| 2008 | Osamu Shimomura | Chemistry |
|------|-----------------|-----------|

"For the discovery and development of the green fluorescent protein, GFP" – shared with Martin Chalfie and Roger Tsien.

**2008**          Makoto Kobayashi                    Physics

*"For the discovery of the origin of the broken symmetry which predicts the existence of at least three families of quarks in nature."*

**2008**          Toshihide Maskawa                   Physics

*"For the discovery of the origin of the broken symmetry which predicts the existence of at least three families of quarks in nature."*

**2008**          Yoichiro Nambu                      Physics

*"For the discovery of the mechanism of spontaneous broken symmetry in subatomic physics."*

**2002**          Masatoshi Koshiba                   Physics

*"For pioneering contributions to astrophysics, in particular for the detection of cosmic neutrinos" – shared with Raymond David Jr. and Riccardo Giacconi.*

**2002**          Koichi Tanaka                       Chemistry

*"For the development of methods for identification and structure analyses of biological macromolecules" and "for their development of soft desorption ionisation methods for mass spectrometric analyses of biological macromolecules" – shared with John Fenn and Kurt Wüthrich.*

**2001**          Ryōji Noyori                        Chemistry

*"For their work on chirally catalysed hydrogenation reactions" – shared with William Knowles and Barry Sharpless.*

| **2000** | Hideki Shirakawa | Chemistry |

*"For the discovery and development of conductive polymers" – shared with Alan MacDiarmid and Alan Heeger.*

| **1994** | Kenzaburō Ōe | Literature |

*"Who with poetic force creates an imagined world, where life and myth condense to form a disconcerting picture of the human predicament today."*

| **1987** | Susumu Tonegawa | Physiology or Medicine |

*"For his discovery of the genetic principle for generation of antibody diversity."*

| **1981** | Kenichi Fukui | Chemistry |

*"For their theories, developed independently, concerning the course of chemical reactions" – shared with Roald Hoffmann.*

| **1974** | Eisaku Satō | Peace |

*Who "as Japanese Prime Minister . . . represented the will for peace of the Japanese people, and . . . signed the nuclear arms Non-Proliferation Treaty (NPT) in 1970." – Peace Prize shared with Seán MacBride.*

| **1973** | Leo Esaki | Physics |

*"For their experimental discoveries regarding tunneling phenomena in semiconductors and superconductors, respectively" – shared with Ivar Giaever and Brian David Josephson.*

| **1968** | Yasunari Kawabata | Literature |

*"For his narrative mastery, which with great sensibility expresses the essence of the Japanese mind."*

| **1965** | Sin-Itiro Tomonaga | Physics |

*"For their fundamental work in quantum electrodynamics, with deep-ploughing consequences for the physics of elementary particles"* – shared with Julian Schwinger and Richard Feynman.

| **1949** | Hideki Yukawa | Physics |

*"For his prediction of the existence of mesons on the basis of theoretical work on nuclear forces."*

Sources: Nobel Foundation, Wikipedia

[**Note:** Shuji Nakamura and Yoichiro Nambu held U.S. citizenship at the time of their award.]

## The Blue Laser Diode

**"Technology has no intrinsic value – it takes on value only when manufacturers like us apply it to the products we make."**
*– Tsuneya Nakamura, former president of Seiko Epson,*
We Were Burning, *by Bob Johnstone*

In October, the 2014 Nobel Prize in Physics was awarded to professors Isamu Akasaki of Meijo University, Hiroshi Amano of Nagoya University, and Shuji Nakamura of the University of California, Santa Barbara (UCSB), for "the invention of efficient blue light-emitting diodes, which has enabled bright and energy-saving white light sources."

Nick Holonyak Jr. invented the red LED while working at General Electric in 1962. Jun-ichi Nishizawa, now a professor emeritus at Tohoku University, developed the green LED in 1971, and Akasaki and Amano the first blue LEDs in 1989. Nakamura's work at Nichia Corp. resulted in increases in brightness and longevity that enabled the commercialization of blue LEDs in 1994. (LEDs were first used in traffic lights in the Japanese cities of Tokushima and Nagoya.) RGB white light could then be created using LEDs, marking the beginning of the end for Edison's incandescent light bulb.

Several other scientists also made important contributions to the development of LED technology, including Jerry Woodall, now a Distinguished Professor at the University of California, Davis.

As a result of Nakamura's discoveries, Nichia became the world's leading producer of LEDs, a position it still held in 2015. But the company paid him only ¥20,000 (currently U.S.$170) for each of the nearly 200 patents he filed while working there. Feeling he'd been taken advantage of, Nakamura resigned from Nichia and in February 2000 joined UCSB. In November of that year, he became a consultant to Cree, America's leading maker of LEDs and LED lighting products. A long and complicated drama ensued, involving patent infringement lawsuits, Nakamura suing for compensation, and the rapid growth of the LED market. Those who are interested the story can read about it in Bob Johnstone's book *Brilliant! Shuji Nakamura and the Revolution in Lighting Technology*. Those interested in the physics may refer to *The Blue Laser Diode: The Complete Story*, by Shuji Nakamura, Stephen Pearton and Gerhard Fasol.

Professor Nakamura is now a citizen of the United States. In 2008, together with professors Steven DenBaars (founder of Nitres, a developer of nitride-based semiconductor devices acquired by Cree in 2000) and James Speck of UCSB's College of Engineering, he founded

SORAA, the only maker of gallium nitride LEDs on gallium nitride substrates. GaN on GaN LEDs emit more light, are more efficient, and have other advantages compared with LEDs built on silicon carbide or sapphire substrates. White LED lighting already accounts for the majority of residential and commercial lighting sales in Japan, and worldwide sales are estimated by analysts and industry sources to have risen by as much as 90% in 2014, to account for nearly 10% of total general lighting demand.

## Regenerative Medicine

In July 2013, Japan's Health, Labor and Welfare Ministry approved the world's first clinical research using induced pluripotent stem (iPS) cells from a patient's own body. Proposed by the Institute of Physical and Chemical Research (Riken), the project aims to use iPS cells to halt and possibly reverse macular degeneration of the retina, a common cause of vision problems for elders.

The purpose of the research, which is being conducted at the Institute of Biomedical Research and Innovation in Kobe, is to confirm the safety of the cells and their surgical transplantation. The project is an outgrowth of research conducted by Kyoto University professor Shinya Yamanaka, who shared the 2012 Nobel Prize in Physiology or Medicine with Sir John B. Gurdon for their discovery that "mature, specialised cells can be reprogrammed to become immature cells capable of developing into all tissues of the body."

In March 2014, Yamanaka announced that iPS cells would be provided to Riken, Keio University, Osaka University, and other research institutions in Japan, with the first three assessing their suitability for the treatment of eye disease, spinal cord injuries, and heart disease, respectively. Yamanaka also hopes to lower the cost of treatment by using iPS cells made from the blood cells of different people chosen for their small chance of rejection. Also in March 2014, a research team lead by Kyoto University professor Jun Takahashi announced progress in developing a treatment for Parkinson's disease using iPS cells. Clinical tests of the treatment are scheduled to begin in 2016.

Supporting biomedical research and the development of Japan's medical and pharmaceutical industries is a priority of the Abe government, which plans to create Japanese equivalents of the U.S. National Institutes of Health. In July 2013, the Japanese Health Ministry and the U.S. Food and Drug Administration announced plans to "unify standards for screening the safety and effectiveness of regenerative medicine based on induced pluripotent stem cells" (*Nikkei*, July 10, 2013).

# III.

# From Mercantilism to Comparative Advantage

"The myth of MITI – Japan's Ministry of International Trade and Industry – is as dubious as it is durable. According to the myth, a prescient group of bureaucrats at MITI planned, designed, guided, and funded Japan's efforts in chips and computers, using and coordinating the resources of Japan's huge business organizations along the way.

"This vision is about as true as Japan's counterclaim that still larger Pentagon subsidies explain the success of Silicon Valley."

*– George Gilder,*
Microcosm: The Quantum Revolution
in Economics and Technology

In his highly influential book *MITI and the Japanese Miracle: The Growth of Industrial Policy, 1925–1975* (Stanford University Press, 1982), the late American professor and Asian studies scholar Chalmers Johnson analyzed the leading role of Japan's economic bureaucracy in the country's high-speed industrialization. He described the development of industrial policy as Japan attempted to catch up with the Western imperialists who had forced the opening of the country, the shift from light to heavy industries, the development of the Ministry of International Trade and Industry (MITI) out of the old Ministry of Munitions, and MITI's use of the Japan Development Bank to guide economic recovery after WWII.

Johnson's meticulous scholarship has shaped the thinking of countless students, scholars, and policymakers ever since. For those interested in the workings of the Japanese government, his book *Japan: Who Governs?: The Rise of the Developmental State* (W.W. Norton & Co., 1996) is also recommended.

But *MITI and the Japanese Miracle*, as Bob Johnstone pointed out in *We Were Burning*, is a dated book containing very little discussion of electronics, and MITI has a mixed record of helping, hindering, directing, and failing to direct companies in the electronics, auto, and other industries.

It is also important to note that in addition to promoting industries targeted for growth, Japan's economic bureaucracy has helped – and continues to help – coordinate the consolidation of industries such as petrochemicals and oil refining that have gone into structural decline, scaling back what it once worked to build up. However, it was the case that a combination of industrial guidance, an undervalued exchange rate, regulation, and nationalist attitudes restrained imports and promoted exports into the 1980s, and the competitiveness generated thereby supported a structural trade surplus until 2011 (excluding deficits resulting from the first and second oil shocks).

Some of the non-tariff barriers were amusing (e.g., Japan cannot import European skis because Japanese snow has different qualities; Japanese people cannot digest American rice because they have longer intestines), but many of the consequences – including the decline of the American steel, machine tool, and consumer electronics industries – were not. That having been said, MITI's policies would have accomplished very little without the entrepreneurship and technical abilities of Japanese industry, as well as the active participation of the American government and American corporations in Japan's postwar economic recovery and subsequent development.

It is ironic that Koreans, Taiwanese, and Chinese have used Japanese tactics to do to Japan what Japan did to America. Japan, in turn, has lost its dominance of the steel, shipbuilding, and consumer electronics industries, while Japanese corporations have found it very difficult to prevent the outflow of technology to their Asian rivals and even their own Asian business partners.

China's high-speed trains were built using technology taken from Kawasaki Heavy Industries and other Japanese companies, which China then claimed as its own. In March 2014, Toshiba sued Korean memory chipmaker SK Hynix for allegedly stealing trade secrets related to NAND flash memory, which Toshiba had invented. Toshiba's American joint venture partner SanDisk has done the same. The IP was allegedly transferred to SK Hynix by a Japanese employee of SanDisk.

This was not the first such incident: in 2004, Toshiba sued Hynix for violation of its semiconductor patents. The issue was eventually settled through a licensing agreement, in 2007. Toshiba's official statement read: "Moving forward, Toshiba will construct a more robust system for protecting its intellectual property and preventing its loss, and respond resolutely to unfair competition."

In December 2014, Toshiba and Hynix reached another settlement, as a result of which Toshiba agreed to withdraw its lawsuit in exchange for a settlement fee. As stated in a Toshiba press release, the two companies also "agreed to expand their relationship by extending existing supply agreements for DRAM and patent cross licensing, and to start collaboration in the development of nano-imprint lithography...."

The press release also noted that "Toshiba will continue to respond resolutely to unfair competition, in order to maintain the advanced technical competence that is the source of its competitive strength."

Better late than never. After decades of evolution, Japan has joined the United States and Europe as a defender of intellectual property rights.

## The Yen

> "It may be recalled that the single exchange rate of 360 yen to the dollar was established in April 1949 while Japan was still under the Occupation and also that this rate was judged by many experts then as similar to a handicap given to a convalescent golfer. Quite soon after, the 360-yen rate turned out to be yen-cheap as Japanese manufacturing industries recovered their potential efficiency and further caught up with the front-ranking countries of the West."
>
> – *Shigeto Tsuru,*
> Japan's Capitalism: Creative Defeat and Beyond

The weak yen – perennial complaint of the American auto industry and pet peeve of members of the U.S. Congress from Michigan and certain lobbyists in Washington, DC – was "Made in America." Ironically, one might even say that it was made in Detroit.

By the end of WWII, Japan's economy had collapsed and the country was in a state of desperate chaos, with mass poverty, black markets run by the Yakuza, and runaway inflation. The Cold War was beginning, and the American government was concerned about the rise of left-wing political parties (the Socialists won Japan's first postwar general election) and anxious to turn Japan into a bulwark against communism. Against this setting, the U.S. sent Joseph Morrell Dodge to Tokyo in early 1949 to serve as financial advisor to the Supreme Commander for the Allied Powers, General Douglas MacArthur.

Dodge had been chairman of the Detroit Bank from 1933 to 1953 and had served as financial advisor to the U.S. military government in postwar Germany. He devised a stabilization and revitalization policy for Japan – called "The Dodge Line" – which included balancing the national budget, increasing tax revenues, reducing government intervention in the economy, and fixing the exchange rate at 360 yen to the U.S. dollar in order to promote exports. The policy was successful.

The yen / dollar exchange rate remained at 360 for more than 20 years, until 1971, when the U.S. went off the gold standard. By then, Japan's chronic postwar trade deficit had become a surplus of $5.8 billion. In December of that year, the Smithsonian Agreement set a new rate of 308. The agreement collapsed two years later, and the exchange rates of major currencies were allowed to float.

The sharp appreciation of the yen that followed caused acute anxiety over the viability of Japan's export-led growth strategy, which in turn led to heavy government intervention in currency markets. Despite that intervention, in 1973 the yen rose to 271 to the dollar. It retreated during the first oil crisis, but then – again driven by trade surpluses – rose to 211 in 1978.

In the first half of the 1980s, higher interest rates in the United States more than offset Japan's trade surplus, resulting in capital outflow, a decline in the value of the yen to 239 to the dollar, and further growth of Japan's trade surplus. This led to the Plaza Accord of 1985. Signed by the governments of the United States, Japan, Germany, the United Kingdom, and France at the Plaza Hotel in New York City, the Plaza Accord was an attempt to reduce the U.S. trade deficit through coordinated intervention in the currency markets. The yen appreciated rapidly thereafter, rising to 128 to the dollar in 1988 and 80 to the dollar in 1995.

As Japan's asset bubble inflated in the second half of the 1990s, the yen depreciated, eventually falling to 134 to the dollar in 2002, in conjunction with the sharp decline in electronics exports following the bursting of the Internet bubble. For the next five years, it remained weak due to relatively low interest rates in Japan during an economic recovery led by the United States. This was exacerbated by the carry trade, in which investors borrowed in yen in order to speculate in higher-yielding currencies, and repeated intervention by the Bank of Japan. In 2007, the yen dropped to 123 to the dollar and 170 to the euro (from 89 in 2000).

In the financial and economic crisis triggered by the collapse of Lehman Brothers in 2008, the yen once again appreciated, this time as a safe-haven currency. It peaked at 76 to the dollar in 2011 and 95 to the euro in 2012. In that year, Japan ran a $58.2 billion trade surplus with the United States. Since 1971, the yen had appreciated by 4.7x vs. the dollar, and Japanese products had still not been priced out of the U.S. market.

After the Fukushima Daiichi nuclear disaster in March 2011, Japan's nuclear power plants were shut down, and imports of coal, oil, and natural gas surged, resulting in the first trade deficit in two decades. In 2012, the current account went into deficit. This, plus the expansion of the money supply and massive Japan Government Bond (JGB) purchases under Prime Minister Abe and Bank of Japan governor Haruhiko Kuroda, caused the yen to depreciate by 34% to 102 to the dollar, and by 50% to 143 to the euro, by the end of March 2014. Although these rates were far from the yen's 2007 lows, the depreciation was large enough and fast enough to generate howls of complaints from U.S. automakers and the German industry.

Rates remained near these levels until October, when Kuroda announced another round of quantitative easing. By the end of the year, the yen was at 120 to the dollar and 145 to the euro. This time, most of the protests – which were ignored – came from Korea and other countries in Asia. The Americans, feeling good about economic recovery, and the Europeans, busy with other problems, were mostly silent.

Looking ahead, the decline in oil and other natural resource prices should lead to improvement in the current account and trade balance, which in turn should help support the value of the yen. But a further expansion of the money supply cannot be ruled out.

## Japan's Trade Balance (JPY 100b) vs. JPY/USD 1950–2014

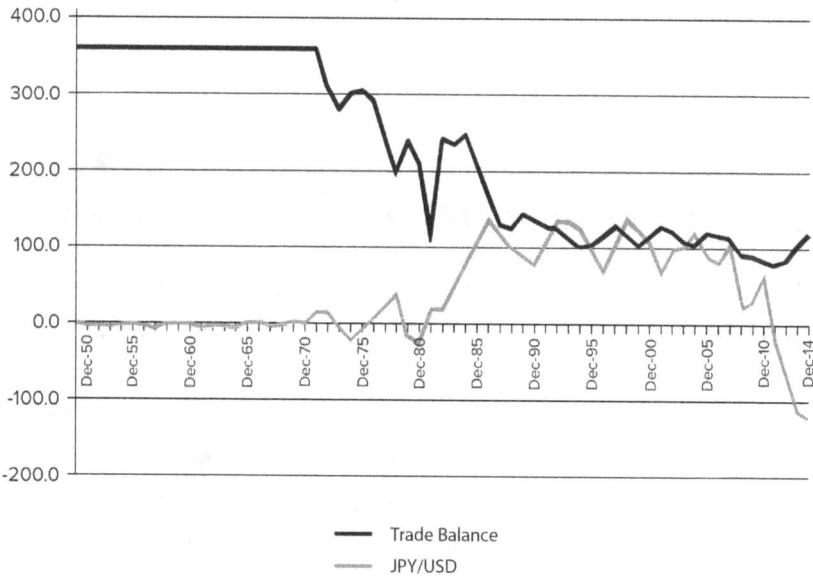

Trade Balance

JPY/USD

Source: Japan Ministry of Finance

## JPY/USD vs. Japan's Current Account & Trade Balance 1996–2014 (JPY 100 billions)

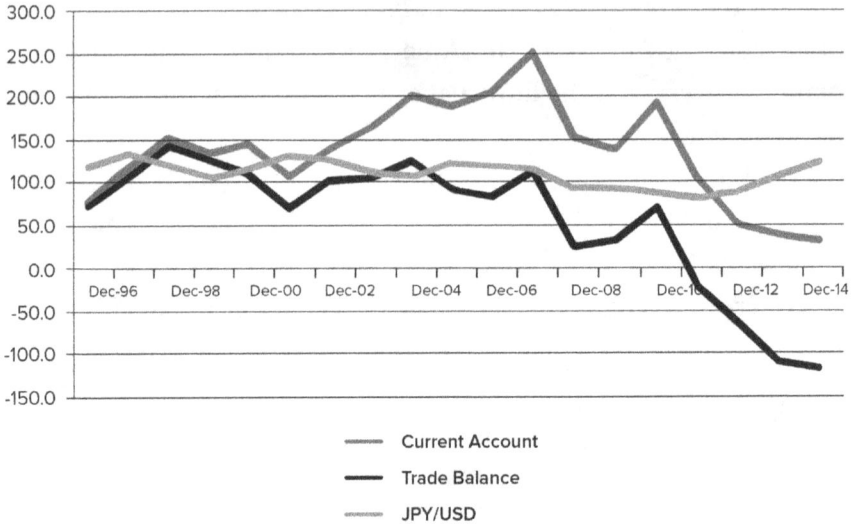

Source: Japan Ministry of Finance

# U.S. Autos: Uncompetitive at Any Exchange Rate?

While the Japanese auto industry has built up a large sales and manufacturing presence in the U.S., the U.S. auto industry has demonstrated little staying power in Japan. Since Japan imposes no tariffs on vehicle imports, Detroit and the U.S. government blame the very small number of American car sales in Japan on what are called *non-tariff barriers*, including vehicle standards, closed sales channels, and tax incentives – in fact, pretty much anything that varies from standard American practice.

The real issues are more pragmatic. For one, the steering wheel of most American cars for sale in Japan (Jeep being an exception) is on the wrong side; Japan is a left-hand-traffic, right-hand-drive country.

The Japanese design different models for the American market, which varies quite a bit from their own, while U.S. automakers generally offer the same cars in Japan that they sell in America. American car dealers tend to sell multiple brands, but Japanese carmakers have their own dealer networks – meaning that to be successful in Japan, a foreign carmaker must establish its own. (One specialized foreign car dealer, Yanase, sells several European and American brands nationwide, with limited success.)

Most American cars are too big for Japanese roads – approximately 40% of the cars sold in Japan are mini-cars (no larger than 3.4m – 11.15 feet – high, 2.0m (6.6 feet) long, and 1.48m (4.9 feet) wide, with 1300cc or smaller engine displacement), which are taxed at lower rates than larger vehicles in order to help reduce fuel consumption. Finally, the quality of American cars either is, or is perceived to be, inferior to that of Japanese cars.

During the first oil shock, small, fuel-efficient Japanese cars took market share in the U.S. Forty years later, despite concerns about pollution and climate change, the American auto industry and the Office of the U.S. Trade Representative (USTR) have called tax preferences for fuel-efficient vehicles in Japan a "non-tariff barrier."

The U.S. imposes a 2.5% tariff on imported passenger cars and a 25% tariff on light trucks, including SUVs. In addition to protecting American jobs and auto industry profits, this is an ecologically sound policy. But if you are American and in favor of free trade, did you know that you might have paid 22.5% more for your SUV than you would have paid if the standard tariff on passenger cars had been applied?

As difficult as it is to sell foreign cars in Japan, it is possible to buy Japanese automakers. Today, the most prominent example of this is the Renault-Nissan Alliance, formed in 1999 to enable Renault's highly effective CEO, Carlos Ghosn, to save Nissan from bankruptcy. Renault now owns 43.4% of Nissan (with full voting rights), while Nissan owns 15% (non-voting) of Renault.

Beginning in 1971, General Motors acquired stakes in Isuzu, Suzuki, and Fuji Heavy Industries (generally known by its brand name, Subaru) that eventually amounted to 49%, 20%, and 20%, respectively. By 2008, faced with bankruptcy, it had sold all these shares. Chrysler bought 15% of Mitsubishi Motors (from which it sourced the Dodge Colt) in 1971, raised its stake to more than 20% in 1988, reduced it to less than 3% in 1992, and then sold it down to zero. Ford Motor Co. bought 7% of Mazda in 1979, raised its stake to 33.3% by 1996, then sold it down to zero by 2010.

And perhaps selling out was the right thing to do. Today the Japanese auto market is crowded, low-margin, and shrinking. Focusing on the larger and growing Chinese market – which General Motors is doing – makes a lot more sense.

While this was happening, the Japanese built a large manufacturing presence in North America, and exports from these factories are now starting to overtake imports from Japan. In 2013, Honda exported 23% more vehicles from North America than it shipped to North America from Japan, those exports going to some 50 countries. Toyota is headed in the same direction: it ships its Highlander SUV from Indiana to Australia, New Zealand, Russia, and Ukraine. Nissan is also shifting production from Japan to North America.

Meanwhile, foreign automakers are gradually increasing their market shares in Japan. Imports accounted for 8.5% of vehicle registrations in 2013, and industry sources expect them to reach 10% in the near future. Japanese government statistics for 2013 show total unit imports of foreign cars up 5.1%, with imports from Europe up 23.3% and imports from America down 4.3%. Visits to foreign car dealerships in Tokyo reveal the reason for the disparity: many more European models are available, they are not too large for Japanese roads, and European steering wheels are on the right-hand side of the car. Evidently, the Japanese also find their design more appealing: BMW's MINI Cooper is a common site on Japanese roads.

Foreign cars are relatively expensive in Japan. Ford has launched a 1.0 liter Fiesta there for a little more than ¥2 million (USD $24,000). A two-seater electric Smart car sells for about JP¥4 million. We paid JP¥850,000 for our 1.3-liter gasoline-powered Toyota Passo. The most fuel-efficient Japanese gasoline-powered mini-cars now get more than 30km per liter (70 miles per gallon), and vehicles with better mileage are on the way.

## Tesla Gets Japan

European automakers have established themselves in Japan through a combination of technology and style, but Tesla Motors is the only American automaker to bring something new and better to Japan in recent decades, the only one that has taken a meaningful share of the Japanese imagination, and perhaps the only one that has what it takes to succeed in Japan.

Tesla's Tokyo showroom, opened in 2010, is located across the road from Oracle Japan, on Aoyama-Dori, in one of the city's more fashionable districts. Tesla representatives there and in Osaka say that test drives have been booked solid, leading to hundreds of advance orders for the Model S. They say they have had no problems on long-distance test drives to check the vehicle's 265-mile (426.5km) certified single-charge range.

There are almost 50 high-power (200V) charging points for Tesla electric vehicles in Japan – from Fukuoka, in Kyushu, to Sendai, north of Fukushima – and many more ordinary charging stations located throughout the country. The batteries are made by Panasonic, which reportedly may invest close to U.S.$1 billion in Tesla's planned "gigafactory," which will make batteries for the mass-market electric car that Tesla plans to launch in 2017. Tesla also works with, and has received investments from, Toyota and Daimler-Benz.

## Japan Reaches Its Limits

"…[T]he strength of government intervention has not been the decisive factor behind Japan's success.…everything that has occurred in this country has stemmed ultimately from the cumulative strength of the people themselves."

– *Makoto Kikuchi, Sony Research Director,*
Japanese Electronics: A Worm's Eye-View of its Evolution

Not to mention the opportunity presented by the United States.

The transistor was invented at Bell Telephone Laboratories (later called AT&T Bell Laboratories, or simply Bell Labs) in 1947. In 1949 – the same year Joseph Dodge went to Tokyo to straighten out the Japanese economy – the U.S. Department of Justice brought an antitrust suit against AT&T as a result of which, in 1956, the company was obliged to license all its patents to American companies for free and to foreign companies that paid royalties. Two years later, the Justice Department ruled that RCA and its David Sarnoff Research Center would have to license its TV patents to other American companies free of charge. Choosing not to compete in overseas markets, RCA sold its technology to foreign companies, most of them Japanese.

Also in 1947, the American statistician William Edwards Deming arrived in Japan to work with the Occupation. Taking the opportunity to promote his method of statistical quality control, he predicted that the quality of Japanese products, which was then derided as inferior, would soon be the best in the world. Japanese corporations introduced what they called "Quality Control (QC) circles" and made the prediction come true. The Deming Prize, established in 1951 and administered by the Japanese Union of Scientists and Engineers, is now one of the world's most respected quality management awards.

In October 1953, Sony had arranged to license transistor technology from Western Electric, but without asking MITI for permission in advance. When Sony applied for $25,000 in U.S. currency to complete the transaction, MITI was furious at the breach of protocol and did not release the funds until February 1954. As a result, Sony missed launching the world's first transistor radio by a month, beaten by Texas Instruments.

By 1960, RCA had licensed TV and other patents to more than 80 Japanese companies. In that year, David Sarnoff, as head of RCA, visited Japan. He was met at the airport by Prime Minister Ikeda, given the keys to the city by the governor of Tokyo, and presented with the Order of the Rising Sun by the emperor. At the time, it was estimated that Japan accounted for about 80% of RCA's royalty income, with revenues amounting to U.S.$200 million to $300 million per year.

These and other developments in the postwar years lay the groundwork for Bob Johnstone's book *We Were Burning*. Johnstone is an Australian writer who, as a journalist covering the rise of the Japanese electronics industry in the 1980s and 1990s, collected the stories of the inventors and entrepreneurs who made it happen. He does not concern himself with the economic policies that were used by the Japanese government to promote the electronics industry.

Moving through the origin and development of transistors, integrated circuits, image sensors, LEDs, LCDs, electronic calculators, digital watches, camcorders, music synthesizers, CD players, printers, LED lighting, and other products, the book's common themes are Japanese engineers and entrepreneurs adopting and improving on the technologies made available by the American legal system and American managerial decisions, and by American inventors frustrated by lack of support from American corporate management who found enthusiastic partners in Japan. A great read and necessary counterpoint to *MITI and the Japanese Miracle*, *We Were Burning* is now also showing its age.

Dedicated to "making things" (*monozukuri*), the Japanese were unable to grasp the concept of the fabless (no factories) IC design company, slow to appreciate the significance of the Internet, and unable to compete with American software (game software being the exception that proves the rule); unable to conceive of the combination of hardware, software, and Web-based applications created by Apple; and unable to match American venture capital or compete with the aggressive pricing and investment strategies of the best Korean and Taiwanese companies in commoditized digital electronics.

Personal encounters in Japan illustrate the situation. Back in the 1990s, a senior manager at a major Japanese PC maker told me: "As a maker [of things], we find it difficult to understand how a company such as Microsoft can make so much money." Sleepless in Seattle, Clueless in Tokyo.

More recently, when I told representatives of a Japanese cell phone maker that I thought the iPhone was a very good product, one of them said, "Of course it is. It's full of Japanese components." In a karaoke bar in the back streets of Kyoto, a Japanese fund manager severely criticized the products and strategies of Japanese cell phone makers, then pulled out his iPhone and said, "They've forgotten what it means to be Japanese. This is Japanese." Steve Jobs might have thought the same. Apple now has almost half of the Japanese cell phone market.

Faced with competition they are not equipped to deal with, Japanese manufacturers have fallen back on the original sources of their competitive advantage: high-precision machinery (including semiconductor production equipment, chip mounting assembly equipment, machine tools, medical equipment, and analytical instruments), high-quality miniaturized components (including NAND flash memory, microcontrollers, capacitors, image sensors, optical lenses, batteries, displays, precision motors, and industrial sensors), and advanced industrial materials (including metals, chemicals, and films). When the Tohoku earthquake and Thailand floods wrecked Japanese factories in 2011, their customers, including the Asian competitors of Japan's struggling consumer electronics giants, discovered how dependent they were on Japanese suppliers. They still are.

## iPhone Parts Made by Japanese Manufacturers

| | |
|---|---|
| Touchscreen LCD panel | Japan Display, Sharp |
| Backlights | Minebea, Omron |
| CMOS image sensor | Sony |
| Lithium-ion battery | Sony |
| Electronic compass | Asahi Kasei |
| NAND flash memory | Toshiba |
| DRAM memory | Elpida (subsidiary of Micron) |
| Driver ICs | Renesas |
| Crystal oscillator timing device | Seiko Epson |
| Capacitors | Murata Mfg., Taiyo Yuden |
| WLAN/Bluetooth module | Murata Mfg. |
| Power coils | TDK |
| Transistors | Rohm |
| Resin substrate for mounting parts | Ibiden |

Sources: Nikkei, company information

# Giving Away the Store

"I am more worried that we will have to bail out the economy of Japan than I am about having to protect our technological base."

– *Unnamed official, U.S. Office of Technology Policy, 1989*
*(from* Winner Take All, *by Richard Elkus)*

*Winner Take All: How Competitiveness Shapes the Fate of Nations*, by Richard J. Elkus (Basic Books, 2009), provides a clear and insightful explanation of how the United States lost so much of the electronics, auto, machinery, and other industries to the guided capitalism and mercantilism of Japan and other countries in East Asia. It is an account, by a senior executive who was directly involved, of how top

American management sold, licensed, and outsourced key technologies in pursuit of short-term profit and how Japan – followed by Korea, Taiwan, and China – did not waste the opportunity provided to them.

In 1970, as general manager of the Educational and Industrial Products Division of Ampex Corp., Elkus introduced InstaVideo, the first video cassette recorder (VCR) brought to market. Earlier that year, he was taken to Japan by his CEO to negotiate a joint venture with Toshiba in which Toshiba would manufacture VCRs using technology provided by Ampex. Three years later, on the edge of bankruptcy, Ampex dropped the product, leaving Toshiba with the technology and its mass production facilities. VCRs soon became a monster hit for the Japanese consumer electronics industry, although more for Sony and JVC than for Toshiba.

Commenting on the recovery of Japanese industry after the war, Elkus noted that after the Japanese got back on their feet, helped by the "desire [on the part of the U.S.] to subcontract the production of electromechanical devices [to Japan]...an amazing thing happened:

> Japan's manufacturing expertise...began to grow remarkably innovative....[T]he Japanese showed an ability to create the front end of new product designs. Products and processes began to converge. As they began to integrate these front-end designs with the electromechanical components resulting from their expertise in mass production, the Japanese were able to introduce a multiplicity of highly desirable, relatively inexpensive proprietary products at an exponential rate. At the same time, as front-end designs and manufacturing expertise converged into integrated systems, reliability and ease of operation became a competitive advantage.

The integration was facilitated by Japan's comprehensive and coordinated industrial structure, as well as the Japanese preference for accumulating technologies rather than shuffling portfolios of products and companies.

Elkus identifies 10 principles of competition in a technology-driven world:

1. As end-use products, markets and related technologies evolve, they become increasingly interrelated, interdependent and integrated.
2. Growth of products and markets is always evolutionary, never revolutionary.
3. As the cost of building an infrastructure rises exponentially, the price of reentry to those who have lost that infrastructure becomes overwhelming.
4. The nation's political and economic strategy is primary in establishing its educational agenda. The educational agenda seldom establishes the nation's political and economic strategy.
5. Certain technologies, products, and markets are strategic to a nation's industrial base and ability to compete.
6. Weakness in one sector may cause weakness in dependent sectors.
7. A substantial loss of strategic infrastructure will ultimately impair a nation's ability to develop meaningful economic and political relationships with other nations.
8. Significant losses in the infrastructure of strategic technologies, products, and markets reduce a nation's ability to influence its economic and political destiny.
9. If the nation as a whole is not competitive, it is difficult for any business or industry within that nation to remain competitive.
10. To be competitive, a nation must have a national strategy for competitiveness.

The exposition of point 10 continues:

"There must be a plan in place – supported by laws, policies, and procedures – to leverage a nation's economic and political resources to its advantage throughout the world... Lack of a strategy is also a strategy – but one doomed to failure."

There was another side to the issue of technology transfer as well: the Japanese did not pay any royalties they didn't have to and did what they could to prevent American companies from becoming established in Japan. The most notorious example of this was the case of the integrated circuit (IC). In 1958, Jack Kilby of Texas Instruments demonstrated the first working IC, filing a patent for the device the following year. In 1961, while his patent was still being analyzed, Robert Noyce of Fairchild Semiconductor was awarded a patent for a "unitary circuit" with a more efficient way of connecting the parts. Fairchild produced the first planar silicon IC in 1960. After a prolonged patent dispute, the two companies cross-licensed their IC technology in 1966.

In the meantime, MITI and Japanese industry collaborated to prevent Fairchild and Texas Instruments from establishing production facilities in Japan, forcing them into licensing agreements on terms that turned out to be quite favorable to the Japanese. Fairchild signed an agreement with NEC in 1963. Texas Instruments, after threatening to impose an embargo on the import of Japanese electronics incorporating its technology, reached an agreement with Sony in 1968. In 1989 the Japanese Supreme Court finally recognized the Kilby patent. As a result of this decision, all Japanese IC makers were forced either to pay for the use of the technology or to enter into cross-licensing agreements with Texas Instruments. But they got a free ride for more than 20 years.

We might well ask why the U.S. government did not intervene on behalf of such a strategic and high-growth industry – just as we might ask why it did so little to prevent Huawei from building a global business on the back of telecommunications technology copied from Cisco Systems, and why it has been so slow to counter Chinese hacking of American industry. The answer to the two questions appears to be the same: the "larger relationship" – i.e., geopolitics – was deemed more important in Washington, DC.

In the case of Japan, several measures were indeed taken, including passage of the Omnibus Foreign Trade and Competitiveness Act in 1988, which resulted in Japan being designated as an unfair trading partner. The Structural Impediment Initiative of 1989 led to negotiations over numerous segments of the Japanese economy regarded as closed to American business (forest products, retail, telecommunications satellites, supercomputers, land sales, public works contracts, and others). Agreements were reached which promised much but delivered little, and President Bill Clinton abandoned the Structural Impediments Initiative in 1993. By then, Japan's economy was on the ropes, and the U.S. had moved on.

As we have seen from the decline of NEC – and as we will see again in following sections – "moving on" was probably the right thing to do.

## Farewell to the Ministry of TEL

> **"More important than MITI, however, in bringing American (semiconductor) capital equipment to Japan was the mighty ministry of TEL."**
>
> *– George Gilder,*
> Microcosm: The Quantum Revolution
> in Economics and Technology

Tokyo Electron Laboratories (TEL) was established in 1963 as an importer of equipment from Thermco (diffusion furnaces), Kulicke & Soffa (wire bonders), Electroglas (probers), VEECO (evaporators), and Varian (ion implanters). It established joint ventures to manufacture products in Japan, bought out some of those ventures, expanded its product line, and built up its own manufacturing capacity. By 1986, it was the largest producer of semiconductor capital equipment in the world. Today, it ranks No. 3 after Applied Materials and ASML, with a dominant position in photo-resist coater / developers and high market shares in deposition, etch, wet clean, and probe. TEL is also a leader in the closely related flat-panel display production equipment industry.

But the semiconductor and display production equipment business has been under pressure for the past several years, due to financial crisis and recession on the one hand and consolidation of the customer base on the other. Demand has been uncomfortably weak and development costs high, and the bulk of orders now come from just five companies: Intel, Samsung Electronics, TSMC, Hynix, and the Toshiba / SanDisk partnership. The Japanese semiconductor industry, once the world's largest, is a shadow of its former self – lagging the U.S., Korea, and Taiwan in sales and only slightly ahead of Europe. At the same time, both TEL and Applied Materials face intense competition from more specialized equipment makers, including KLA-Tencor, Lam Research, Dainippon Screen, and Hitachi High-Technologies.

So it was big news, but quickly understood, when in late September 2013 TEL and Applied Materials announced plans to merge. The two companies planned an "all-stock transaction creating a new company as a merger of equals," under which "Applied Materials shareholders would own approximately 68% of the new company and Tokyo Electron shareholders approximately 32%." Tokyo Electron would provide the chairman of the new company (Tetsuro Higashi), while Applied Materials provided the CEO (Gary Dickerson) and CFO (Bob Halliday). Although billed as a merger of equals, one equal looked a lot more equal than the other. The reaction of investors was positive, but the antitrust review by the U.S. Department of Justice went on for more than a year, until finally, at the end of April 2015, the two companies gave up and canceled the agreement. But a precedent had been set: a Japanese national champion could be taken over without opposition from the Japanese government.

In July 2013, Micron, America's only major producer of memory chips, completed its purchase of Elpida, Japan's last surviving maker of Dynamic Random Access Memory (DRAM). The acquisition made Micron the second-largest semiconductor memory maker in the world (behind Samsung Electronics, ahead of Hynix), gave it advanced design and production capacity in Japan and Taiwan, and raised its share of the mobile DRAM market from 5% to 25%.

Elpida became available for purchase when it went bankrupt during the last downturn. Japanese commentators and politicians wrung their hands and moaned about the loss of a key technology, but Japanese banks lacked the nerve to wait out the cycle. Now demand is up, the yen is down, Micron's sales and profits are up, and in November 2014 its share price hit an 11-year high.

It has been almost 30 years since the Japanese drove Intel out of the DRAM market.

DRAM, incidentally, was invented in 1966 by Robert Dennard of the IBM Thomas J. Watson Research Center. He received a patent for the device two years later. In 2014, the Inamori Foundation (established by Kazuo Inamori, the founder of Kyocera, one of Japan's top makers of electronic components), awarded Dr. Dennard the 2014 Kyoto Prize for Advanced Technology for his invention of DRAM and other contributions to the development of the semiconductor industry.

## Robotics Challenge

In December 2013, a Japanese humanoid robot created by Schaft Inc. took first place in the DARPA Robotics Challenge (DRC) trials in Florida. Inspired by Tokyo Electric Power's inability to control the dispersal of radiation during the Fukushima nuclear disaster, the

DRC aims to develop robots that can work in environments too dangerous for human beings.

The Schaft robot scored 27 out of a total of 32 points awarded for performing tasks such as opening a door, closing valves, clearing debris, walking over broken surfaces, climbing stairs and a ladder, cutting through a wall, attaching a hose to a valve, and driving a vehicle. The robots in second and third place scored 20 and 18 points, respectively. The DRC finals were scheduled to take place in June 2015. According to DARPA, "By the time of the DRC Finals, we expect the robots will demonstrate roughly the competence of a two-year-old child, giving them the ability to autonomously carry out simple commands such as 'Clear the debris in front of you' or 'Close the valve.'"

Schaft is a venture company out of the University of Tokyo; the robot design was aided by research carried out at Japan's National Institute of Advanced Industrial Science and Technology. Google bought the company several months before the DRC trials. Japanese government officials and politicians were appalled, but potential Japanese investors, including the public-private Innovation Network Corp. of Japan, had rejected Schaft's requests for funds. The Japanese government is now attempting to persuade Japanese businesses to acquire venture companies.

Meanwhile, another Japanese robotics venture, Cyberdyne Inc., made a successful IPO in March 2014. Cyberdyne, a startup from the University of Tsukuba, makes robotic exoskeleton suits named after HAL, the intelligent computer in *2001: A Space Odyssey*. Cyberdyne's Robot Suit HAL (Hybrid Assistive Limb) is designed to help people undergoing physiotherapy to overcome cerebral, nerve, and muscle disorders and regain the ability to walk. HAL suits have been approved for clinical use in Japan and Germany. Cyberdyne will probably remain Japanese, as Yoshiyuki Sankai, developer of the concept and president of the company, plans to retain 88% of the voting rights.

# The IT Opportunity

"While the Japanese market and Japanese customers wait for the arrival of the next great thing, most entrepreneurs, and even VC firms, focus instead on China and India. I have never understood why, as China and India represent a market that is an order of magnitude less than Japan when it comes to key technologies, like software. Sure, India and China are fast-growing markets, but the current buyers are in Japan. The way I see it: If you are overlooking Japan you might as well overlook the West Coast of the U.S....

"Entrepreneurs should take note that 85% of all enterprise software is still essentially bought in three core markets: the U.S., Japan, and the U.K."

*– Marc Benioff, Chair and CEO, Salesforce.com*
*"Why Japan Matters. And Microsoft Doesn't"*
*(salesforce.com, The Cloudblog)*

Software and other high-tech businesses are generally not on the U.S.-Japan trade agenda because IBM, Microsoft, Apple, Google, PayPal, Qualcomm, Cisco Systems, Applied Materials, KLA-Tencor, Oracle, Salesforce.com, and other American technology companies have been successful in Japan. Microsoft, Apple, Google, Qualcomm, Oracle, and Salesforce.com don't even have serious Japanese competitors.

Oracle – an easily quantifiable case because Oracle Japan is publicly traded – has increased revenues by about 2.5$x$ since 2000 and currently has an operating margin of about 29%. The operating margin of NEC, a major Japanese supplier of software and telecom equipment, is about 4%. The iPhone and Android handsets each have about 48% of the Japanese cell phone market.

Jonathan Epstein, a Tokyo-based high-tech entrepreneur, angel investor, and former representative of PayPal Japan, notes that Japan has an over-supply of physical infrastructure but an under-supply of Internet-based financial infrastructure. The first half of that statement may be a matter of opinion; the second half is a fact, and an opportunity.

And while Japan lags far behind the U.S. in venture capital investment, so does everyone else. In fact, OECD data indicates that Japan ranks second worldwide in the absolute value of such investments. From Softbank to Internet retailer Rakuten, online game companies, corporate sponsors of startups, local incubators, and angel investors, the venture market in Japan is active and growing. Mobile Monday networking events in Tokyo are crowded with foreign and Japanese entrepreneurs. Widespread complaints about the relative lack of funding and Japan's risk-averse business culture (by Prime Minister Abe, among others) are aimed at speeding things up, and as the example of Schaft indicates, if local investors don't step up, foreign investors can.

### Venture Capital Investments by Country (USD billions)

| | |
|---|---|
| U.S.A. (2012) | 26.7 |
| Japan (2011) | 1.6 |
| Canada (2011) | 1.4 |
| Britain (2012) | 0.9 |
| Israel (2012) | 0.9 |
| France (2012) | 0.7 |
| Germany (2012) | 0.7 |
| South Korea (2012) | 0.6 |
| Australia (2012) | 0.3 |
| Sweden (2012) | 0.3 |

Source: OECD

# Hamamatsu Photonics & the History of Television

Modern television is the result of numerous inventions made in nearly a dozen countries – Germany, France, Russia, Hungary, the United States, England, Japan, and others – starting in the 1850s. In Japan, the "father of television" was Professor Kenjiro Takayanagi, who demonstrated the world's first fully electronic television receiver at Hamamatsu Industrial High School (now the Faculty of Engineering at Shizuoka University) using a cathode ray tube (CRT) display in 1926. The CRT was previously called the Braun tube, after Ferdinand Braun, the German scientist who invented it in 1897. Video signals were first displayed on a Braun tube by the Russian scientist Boris Rosing in 1907. The first public demonstration of a working television was made in London in 1925 by the Scotsman John Logie Baird, who used an electro-mechanical imaging system. The first all-electronic television system was built by the American Philo Farnsworth, who established Farnsworth Television and Radio Corp. in 1938 to manufacture and sell the product.

The CRT became the standard television display until the introduction of flat-panel plasma and liquid crystal display (LCD) televisions in the 1980s and 1990s. The first commercial (pocket-size) LCD TV was put on the market by Casio in 1983, to be followed by larger and larger models from Sharp, Sony, other Japanese and eventually Korean, Taiwanese, and Chinese companies. Sales of LCD TVs overtook sales of CRT TVs in 2007. Sony stopped production of its well-known Trinitron CRT TV in 2008.

Professor Takayanagi had a long and illustrious career as an inventor of television-related technologies (120 patents), as head of the Science and Technical Research Laboratories at

NHK (the Japan Broadcasting Corp.), and as the driving force behind the development of color TV and videotape recorders at JVC (Victor Co. of Japan), where he rose to the level of vice president. He and his students also made important contributions to the development of television and related technologies at Toshiba, NEC, Matsushita (Panasonic), Sharp, Anritsu, and other companies.

In 1953, one of Takayanagi's students, Heihachiro Horiuchi, and two of his colleagues founded Hamamatsu TV Co. to develop and commercialize optoelectronics technology. (A predecessor, Tokai Electronic Laboratory, was established in 1948.) But Hamamatsu TV did not make televisions. Rather, it developed photon multiplier tubes – and, over the years, photodiodes; image sensors and photon-detector units; infrared and x-ray sensors; light sources; laser modules; optical components; industrial, microscope, and x-ray cameras; spectrometers; and other related products. The company changed its name to Hamamatsu Photonics in 1983.

Photon multiplier technology was developed in the 1930s in order to make television cameras sensitive enough to be practical. The first documented demonstration of a photon multiplier tube was made in 1934 at RCA, which led the development and commercialization of the device until the company's breakup in the 1980s. RCA's photon multiplier business was purchased by its managers and made part of Burle Industries, which was acquired by Photonis in 2005. Photonis, which remains a leading producer of solid-state photo sensors, stopped making photon multiplier tubes in 2009.

Hamamatsu TV began production of photon multipliers in 1956 and signed a technical support agreement with RCA in 1960. It established operations in the U.S. and Europe in the 1960s and 1970s, began medical and biological research programs in the

1980s and 1990s, and started production in China in 1990. Six years later, its work in the field of nuclear physics was brought to the attention of the public when it supplied 11,200 20-inch photon multiplier tubes to the Super-Kamioka Neutrino Detection Experiment ("Super-Kamiokande") observatory at the Institute for Cosmic Ray Research, University of Tokyo. The director of the project, Masatoshi Koshiba, shared the Nobel Prize for Physics in 2002.

Hamamatsu Photonics now dominates the market for photon multiplier tubes, with a global market share of more than 90%. Its products are used in medical diagnostics, semiconductor inspection, factory automation, high-energy physics, food inspection, water-quality analysis, radiation monitoring, and many other applications. It is also a leading producer of optical semiconductors used in industrial, analytical, communications, camera, and other applications, as well as imaging and measurement instruments. In 2005, the company established the Graduate School for the Creation of New Photonics Industries in Hamamatsu. Every year it holds a Photon Fair to present its most advanced photon-related technologies: www.photonfair.jp/en/.

# IV.

# From Exports to Global Production

In the 1990s, the Japanese economy slowed to a crawl, and the attention of journalists and economists shifted first to the four "Asian Tigers" – South Korea, Taiwan, Hong Kong, and Singapore – and then to China. The seemingly unstoppable growth of the Japanese auto industry in North America and some other positive stories remained, but for the most part Japanese failure was presented in contrast with the success of other Asian countries and the U.S.. Auto factories aside, the already substantial investments of Japanese industry around the world were generally ignored.

However, the expansion of Japanese trade resumed in the second half of the decade, and foreign direct investment by Japanese corporations started to accelerate in 2000. It was at this point that Japan's trade balance and export statistics began to lose their meaning, as the country shifted to a new model of international growth. Japanese corporations began to add most of their new capacity at lower-cost locations overseas; and while the media focused on slowing domestic growth rates, the overseas portion of the Japanese economy kicked into overdrive. The biggest setbacks to the Japanese economy in the past 20 years was, in fact, the recession triggered by the collapse of Lehman Brothers in 2008 and the Tohoku earthquake and Fukushima nuclear disaster in 2011, not the failure of Japan's model of industrial development.

## Japan Nominal GDP 1996–2014 (% change)

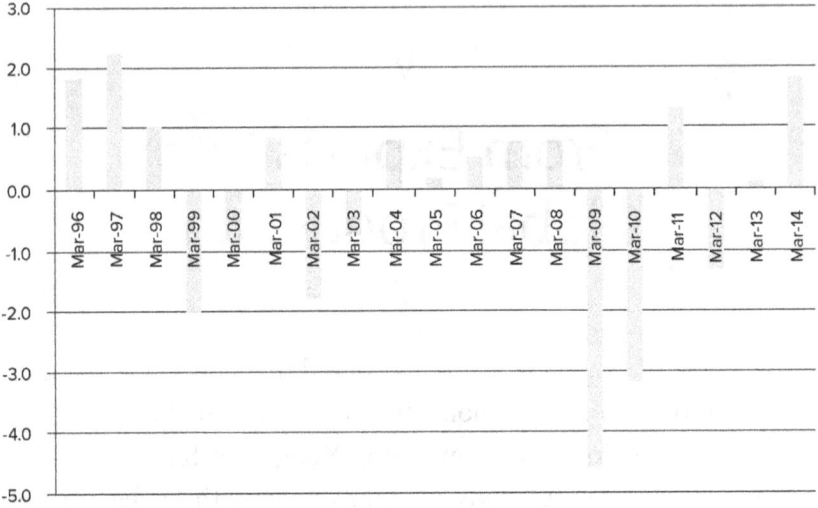

Source: Cabinet Office

## Japan Trade Balance 1964–2014 (JPY billions)

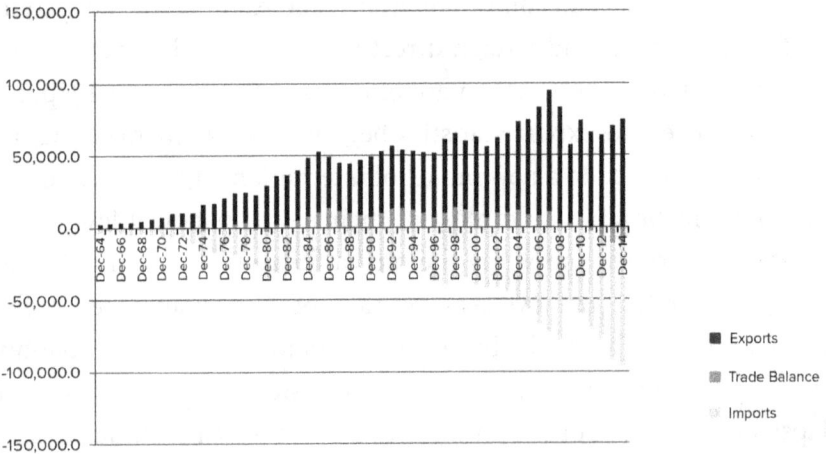

Exports
Trade Balance
Imports

Source: Japan Ministry of Finance

# China: Important, But Not All-Important

The Chinese Communist Party has a concept it calls the "Community of Common Destiny" – a China-centric regional political and economic order that it hopes to build in East and Southeast Asia. Resistance to this concept – combined with territorial disputes, denial of historically documented war crimes by right-wing Japanese politicians, and the Chinese dictatorship's use of Japan as a scapegoat to redirect popular dissatisfaction away from its own failings – has created a great deal of hostility between China and Japan. It has, in fact, almost totally eradicated the good feeling that prevailed when Prime Minister Yukio Hatoyama took office in 2009.

Nevertheless, Japanese exports to China have recovered from the anti-Japanese demonstrations and boycotts orchestrated by the Chinese government in 2012 and the first half of 2013, and Japanese corporations continue to expand their operations in China. It is, therefore, worth having another look at the economic relationship between the two countries.

What we see is that: 1) Japan's exports to China are roughly equivalent to its exports to North America (China accounting for a bit less and North America a bit more than 20% of the total); 2) Japan's imports from China are roughly double its imports from North America; 3) Japan's trade with China is roughly in balance; and 4) after more than tripling in the decade leading to 2011, Japan / China trade has leveled off, at least temporarily. China is attempting to emulate South Korea and do to Japan what Japan did to the U.S., but with limited success so far. This is partly because Japan is directing more of its foreign direct investment to Southeast Asia and partly because it is very difficult to copy the tacit and unpatented knowledge behind high-precision manufacturing.

Japan's exports to other countries in the Asia-Pacific region are considerably larger than its exports to China, and its imports from those countries are larger than its imports from China. Japan has a large trade surplus with North America; smaller surpluses with Asia-Pacific and Europe; small deficits with Latin America, Africa, and the CIS; and a large deficit with the Middle East.

Clearly, the basic pattern is due to Japan being a manufacturing economy with insufficient domestic supplies of energy, raw materials, and food, but it is also worth noting that: 1) despite being a high-wage manufacturing economy, Japan does not have a large structural trade deficit with China; and 2) Japan imports about the same amount from Europe as it does from North America, but its exports to Europe are one-third smaller. These two factors can be attributed to the maintenance of high value-added manufacturing bases in Japan, Germany, and other parts of northern Europe, and America's unique willingness to outsource industrial production. It is also fair to say that the Japanese economy is too big and too globalized to fit inside China's Community of Common Destiny.

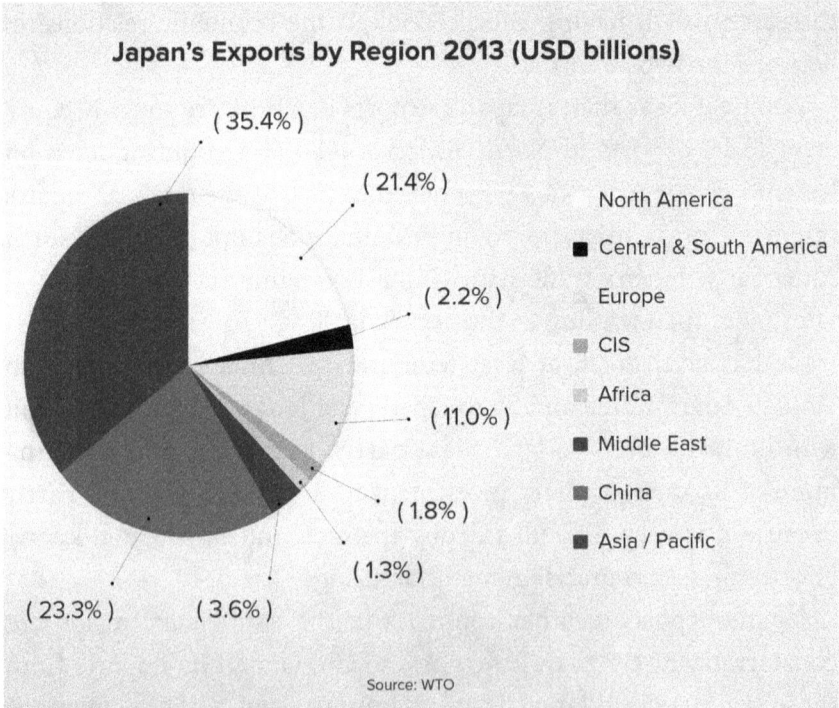

**Japan's Exports by Region 2013 (USD billions)**

( 35.4% )

( 21.4% )

( 2.2% )

( 11.0% )

( 1.8% )

( 1.3% )

( 23.3% )          ( 3.6% )

North America

■ Central & South America

Europe

▨ CIS

▦ Africa

■ Middle East

■ China

■ Asia / Pacific

Source: WTO

## Japan's Imports by Region 2013 (USD billions)

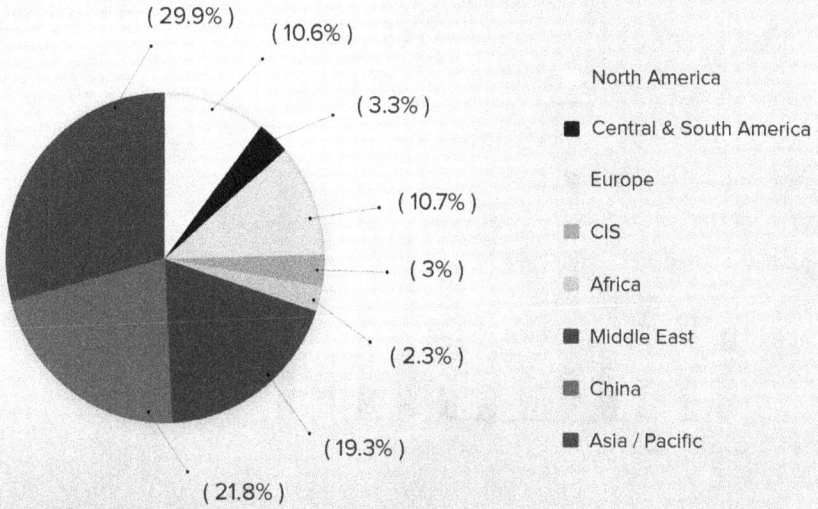

( 29.9% )
( 10.6% )
( 3.3% )
( 10.7% )
( 3% )
( 2.3% )
( 19.3% )
( 21.8% )

North America

■ Central & South America

Europe

▨ CIS

▨ Africa

■ Middle East

▨ China

■ Asia / Pacific

Source: WTO

## Japan's Exports by Region 2002–2013 (USD billions)

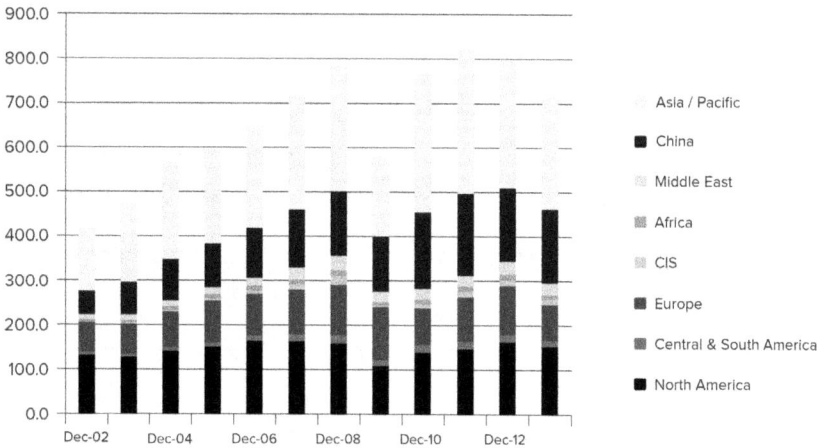

Asia / Pacific

■ China

▨ Middle East

▨ Africa

▨ CIS

■ Europe

■ Central & South America

■ North America

Source: WTO

## Japan's Imports by Region 2002–2013 (USD billions)

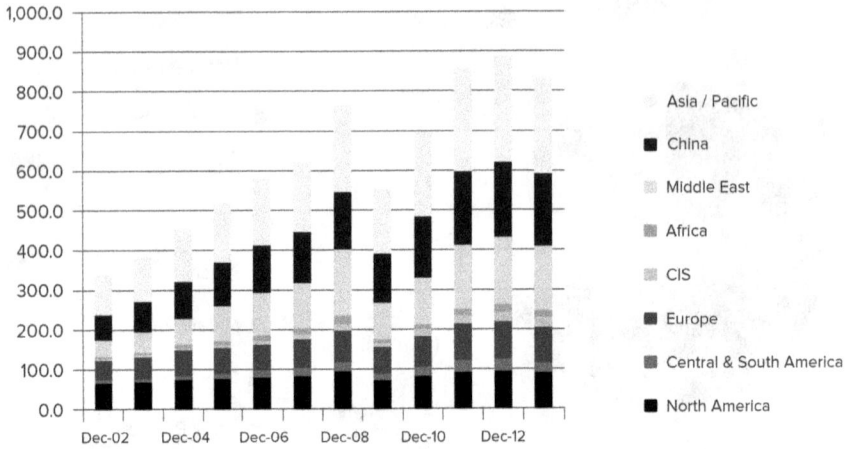

Source: WTO

## Japan's Net Exports 2013 (USD billions)

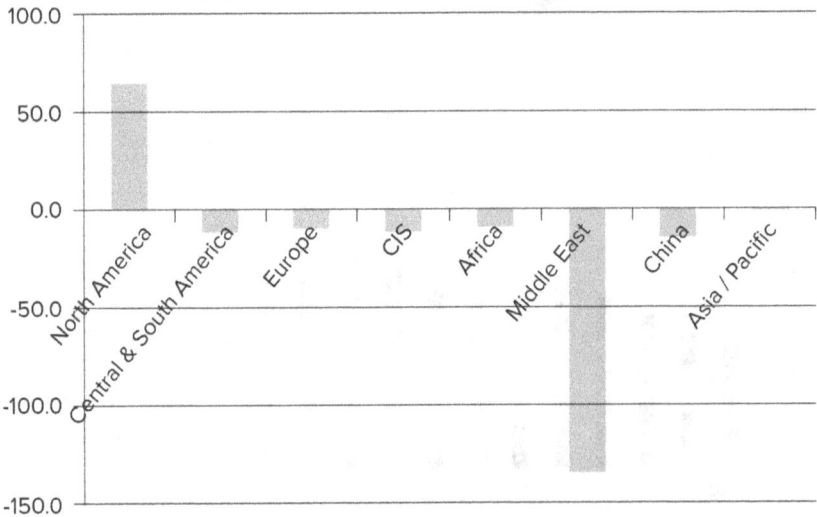

Source: WTO

## Japan's Trade Balance with China 2002–2013 (USD billions)

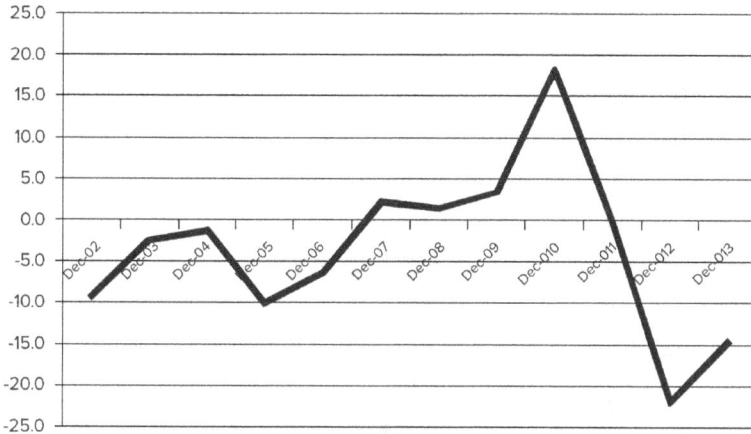

Sources: WTO, Japan Ministry of Finance

# Foreign Direct Investment

Japan's foreign direct investment (FDI) statistics also show China playing a large, but far from dominant, role in the Japanese economy. Although Japan is China's largest source of FDI, China (including Hong Kong) accounts for only 11% of Japan's overseas investments. China accounts for nearly 40% of Japanese FDI in Asia, but that is still less than Japanese FDI in ASEAN (the Association of Southeast Asian Nations). More than half of Japan's outward-bound FDI has gone to NAFTA and the European Union.

For several years now – starting well before the Chinese rioted against Japanese business and boycotted Japanese products in 2012 – Japanese manufacturers have been diversifying their investments away from China to other countries in Asia where wages are lower and there is less risk of their intellectual property being stolen.

Japan's investments in other regions are relatively small. It is interesting to note that its financial investments in the Cayman

Islands exceed its investments in Brazil, India, Russia, the Middle East, Africa, and even Korea and Taiwan. Japan's offshore financial investments have recently attracted a lot of attention due to the 2011 Olympus scandal and the fraudulent mismanagement of pension funds, putting a damper on offshore financial activities. Investments in the Cayman Islands dropped by 19.1% in 2013, falling from 5.7% to 4.3% of Japan's cumulative outward FDI.

Japan is a large net exporter of capital, much of which is invested in hard assets. At the end of 2013, Japanese companies' cumulative outward FDI was 6.5x greater than total FDI in Japan – up from a 3.7x differential a decade earlier. During that 10-year period, inward FDI increased by 90%, while outward FDI expanded by 3.3x. These investments, which may now be in excess of U.S.$1.2 trillion, are usually ignored by commentators bemoaning the state of Japan's national balance sheet.

## Japan's Cumulative Outward Foreign Direct Investment (end 2013)

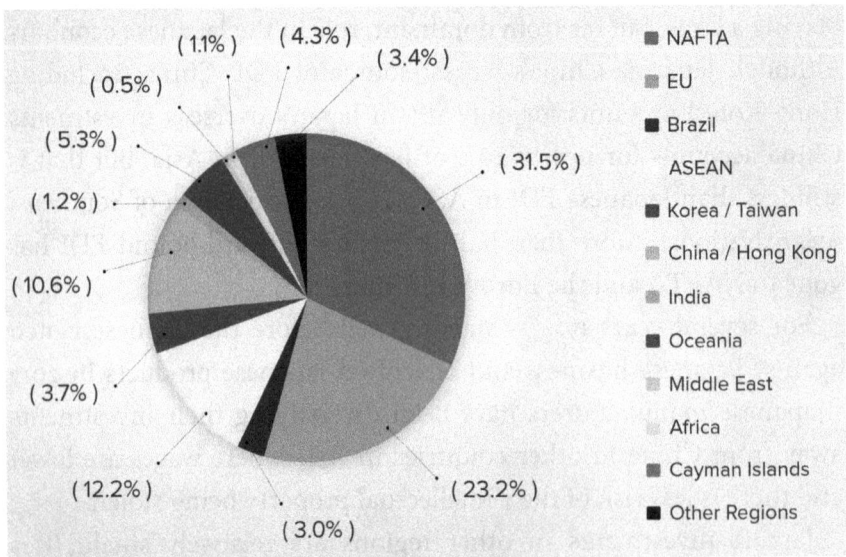

Sources: JETRO, Japan Ministry of Finance

## Japan's Outward vs. Inward
## Foreign Direct Investment 1996–2013 (USD billions)

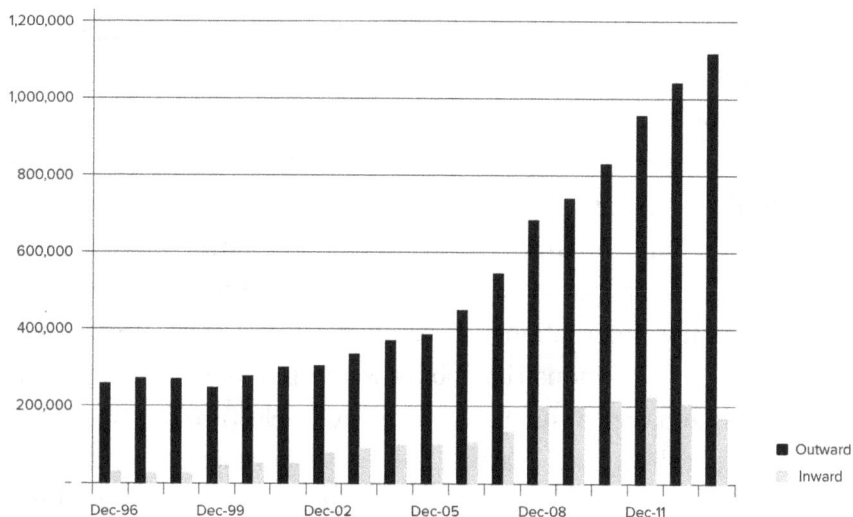

Sources: JETRO, Japan Ministry of Finance

# Automating China: Japanese Industrial Robots

One of China's most serious problems is how to maintain the competitiveness of its manufactured exports and build a more advanced industrial economy while wages are rising at double-digit annual rates and foreign companies are moving assembly operations to cheaper locations in Southeast Asia and elsewhere. Japanese makers of industrial machinery and automation equipment are helping China solve this problem, which helps Japan avoid a structural trade deficit with China in the process.

Japanese exports to China include steelmaking, plastic injection molding, welding, painting, machining, chip mounting, materials handling, and various other types of machinery and equipment – but the most graphic example of what's going on is industrial robots.

There are four major producers of industrial robots in the world –
Fanuc and Yaskawa Electric from Japan, Kuka from Germany, and
ABB from Switzerland – and a long list of others, many of them from
Japan. These include makers of robots themselves (e.g., Kawasaki
Heavy Industries and Nachi-Fujikoshi) and makers of components
such as computerized numerical control equipment (Mitsubishi
Electric) and precision gears (Harmonic Drive Systems, Nabtesco,
and Sumitomo Heavy Industries).

In 2013, China became the world's largest buyer of industrial
robots; in 2014, it moved further ahead. According to preliminary
data from the International Federation of Robotics (IFR), total
worldwide sales of industrial robots were up about 15% in 2014 to
more than 200,000 units. Sales to the auto, electronics, metal and
machinery, rubber and plastics, food and beverage, and pharmaceutical industries all increased. Sales were up about 37% in China
to 50,000 units, accounting for nearly 25% of the total; up 12% in
Japan to 28,000 units; up 10% in South Korea to 23,500 units; up 11%
in Europe to 44,000 units; and up 11% in the Americas to 33.7 units.
Sales in Japan bounced back from a 12% decline in 2013 as the weak
yen prompted manufacturers to increase domestic production.

More than one-half of the industrial robots sold in 2014 were made
by Japanese companies, and Japan remained the world's largest user
of industrial robots, with more than 300,000 units in operation (21%
of the total). Chinese robot makers have yet to establish themselves
in the global market. Western commentators often equate the rise
of China with the decline of Japan, but in fact Japan is enabling the
rise of China while China is supporting the growth of Japan's capital
goods industries.

## Industrial Robots: Annual Shipments (1,000 units)

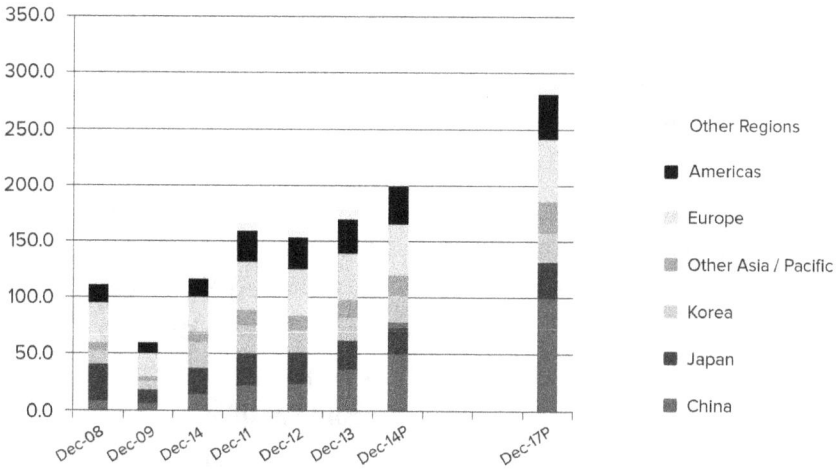

Sources: IFR, World Robotics; ResearchInChina.com

## Industrial Robots: Operational Stock (2014P)

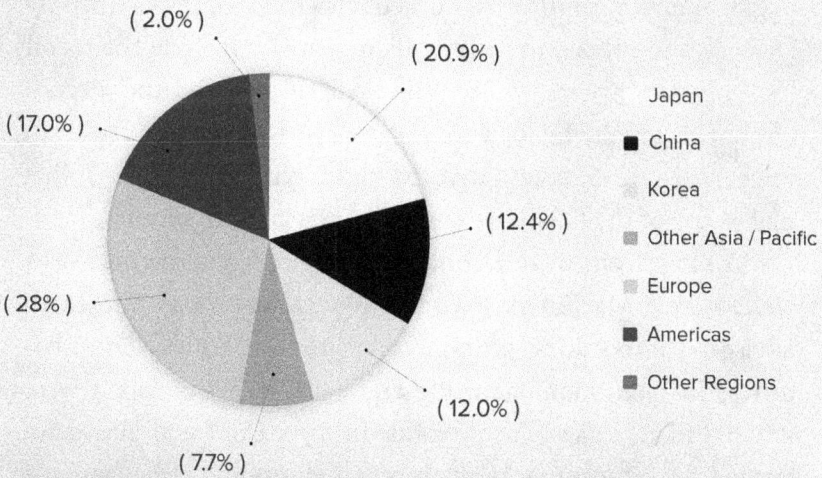

Sources: IFR, World Robotics

# Harmonic Drive Systems

"How did the HarmonicDrive® become what it is today? I believe it is because here in Japan, we became infatuated with the technology, turning the unconventional into the conventional by means of superior design and manufacturing advances. Moreover, it is the result of the hard efforts by numerous customers toward its practical application. I think it can even be said that our customers, by setting such a high bar for manufacturing requirements and problem-solving, have fostered the growth of these products and of us as a company."

– *Yoshihide Kiyosawa, Director, Engineering and R&D,*
*Harmonic Drive Systems*

Clarence Walton (C.W.) Musser (1909-1998) was an American engineer and inventor who worked with the U.S. Department of Defense and private industry. His inventions include the recoilless rifle (co-invented with William Kroeger) and the aircraft ejection catapult. In 1957, he introduced the concept of strain wave gearing, an alternative to rigid gear mechanisms that makes use of the flexibility of metal and elastic dynamics.

Musser's strain wave technology was first commercialized by United Shoe Machinery (USM), where Musser was a research advisor. The resulting gear mechanisms were called *harmonic drives*. In 1964, manufacturing and sales rights in Japan were granted to Hasegawa Gear Works. In 1970, USM and Hasegawa formed a joint venture in Japan called Harmonic Drive Systems. USM also established its own Harmonic Drive division in the U.S.

By the end of the 1990s, Hasegawa and USM had both gone bankrupt, Harmonic Drive Systems was an independent

Japanese-owned company, and USM's Harmonic Drive division had been bought by Nabtesco, another Japanese company. In 2006, Nabtesco transferred its U.S. harmonic drive business to a joint venture 51%-owned by Harmonic Drive Systems. In Europe, Harmonic Drive Systems owns 35% of Harmonic Drive AG, its distributor and manufacturing partner in Germany.

Harmonic drives are used in the joints of industrial robots, machine tools, semiconductor and flat-panel display manufacturing equipment, printing equipment, aerospace, and other applications. Major customers include Hon Hai (Foxconn), the world's largest electronics contract manufacturing company; industrial robot makers Fanuc and Yaskawa Electric; machine tool and robot maker Nachi-Fujikoshi; Mitsubishi Electric' Panasonic; Fuji Machine; Tokyo Electron; and several other leading makers of semiconductor production equipment.

Harmonic drive technology is covered by more than 70 patents awarded to C.W. Musser, and by many others awarded to engineers working for Harmonic Drive Systems. Competition is with other types of gears made by companies in Asia, North America, and Europe. The greatest threat to HDS may come from China, where local companies are attempting to copy the harmonic drive and where patents may not reflect the true origin of the technology. But it seems most likely that HDS will establish its own production facilities in China and that competing with its experience, quality, and economies of scale will be extremely difficult.

In 2006, a Musser Memorial Room was opened on the site of Harmonic Drive Systems' Hotaka Plant in Nagano Prefecture, Japan. Items on display include machine tools and measurement instruments used by Musser; his papers, patent materials, and prototypes around the time he invented the harmonic drive; and other memorabilia presented to the company by his surviving family.

## Separating Politics & Economics

When Prime Minister Abe went to Yasukuni Shrine in December 2013 to pay his respects to Japan's war dead, the visit was widely expected to trigger another Chinese boycott of Japanese goods and perhaps another round of state-sponsored anti-Japanese rioting. But that didn't happen. Press reports from China and Japan suggested that: a) Chinese executives want to maintain and expand profitable trade and investment relations with Japan; b) faced with a slowing economy, Chinese politicians don't want to make the situation worse; and c) China needs Japan's help to solve its pollution problem. In addition, China may want to avoid driving Japan totally into the arms of the U.S.

Whatever the reasons, recent indications are that the environment for Japanese companies operating in China is improving and that many of them are expanding production, sales networks, and R&D there. Meanwhile, the political shouting match between the two countries' leading politicians remains acrimonious.

In early June 2014, a 200-person delegation from 22 Hitachi Group companies met with a similar number of economic policymakers, senior managers from state-owned corporations, and representatives of regional governments in Beijing to discuss what China needs in the areas of infrastructure, energy, and environmental and information technology. The delegation emphasized that Hitachi plans to establish a management structure with decision-making powers in China rather than directing everything from Tokyo. The company plans to increase its R&D staff in China by one-third to 3,000 by the end of FY March 2016. It is already working on smart city projects in Tianjin, Guangzhou, Dalian, and Chongqing.

Hitachi's annual sales in China – which include electrical machinery, elevators, auto parts, and ATMs – now exceed ¥1 trillion (U.S. $10 billion), making the country Hitachi's largest single market outside Japan. According to the *Nikkei*, the Hitachi delegation was invited to Beijing in response to the U.S. Department of Justice indictment of five Chinese military officers for cyber espionage. The Japanese evidently think they now have a chance to break IBM's hold on sales of IT infrastructure to the Chinese government and state-owned corporations. European companies including Siemens, ABB, and Daimler are also reportedly trying to take advantage of the situation. They may, of course, find themselves on the receiving end of similar Chinese manipulations in the future, but this does not seem to be happening yet.

In April 2014, environmental officials from Japan, China, and South Korea met in the South Korean city of Daegu to discuss the air pollution, mostly from China, that affects all three countries, as well as the environmental technology that China would like to receive from Japan and South Korea. The leaders of the three delegations also signed a Joint Communiqué affirming their intention to collaborate in dealing with a "wide range of environmental challenges including water pollution, marine litter, dust and sandstorms, chemical risks, climate change, and biodiversity loss." Japan's Minister of the Environment, Nobuteru Ishihara, told the press, "We had very productive discussions despite the complicated diplomatic relations surrounding the three countries."

## Huge Potential with India

"Japan has spent the last 40 years helping China's rise; it can spend the next 40 years helping India's rise, confident that it will benefit a friend rather than feed a hostile neighbor."

*– Professor David Arase,*
*Hopkins-Nanjing Center for Chinese and American Studies,*
*Nanjing University*

More sensational issues – anti-Japanese riots in China, the dispute over the Senkaku Islands, China's bully-and-grab policy in the South China Sea – have dominated Asian headlines over the past two or three years, but the big new trend in Asia, likely to last for decades, is Japan-India cooperation.

The Japanese and Indian economies are complementary and, when combined, nearly the same size as the Chinese economy, with a larger population and perhaps more growth potential because India is coming from a lower base. India needs Japanese investment, technology, and organizational skills; Japan needs new markets and a lower-cost manufacturing base. As David Arase, quoted above, notes:

> Japan-India bilateral relations are notably trouble-free. There are no zero-sum ideological, territorial, economic, or strategic conflicts to divide them. Factors drawing them together include long-standing mutual admiration and respect for each other's culture, memories of cooperation and mutual support in the modern era, complementary economies, shared democratic values, and parallel global and regional interests.
>
> – *"India-Japan Strategic Partnership in Southeast Asia"*
> (FPRC Journal, 2012 (4), Foreign Policy
> Research Centre, New Delhi)

The expanding Japan-India relationship is also supported by good relations with the United States, ASEAN, and Australia, and by the interest of all three in defending the international order – particularly free maritime trade through the South China Sea and the generally recognized (except by China) territorial waters and exclusive economic zones of the littoral states.

In October 2010, India and Japan concluded negotiations on a Comprehensive Economic Partnership Agreement (CEPA) as part of the India-Japan Strategic and Global Partnership. The statement issued by India's Prime Minister Manmohan Singh and Japan's then-Prime Minister Naoto Kan noted that the CEPA would make use of the two countries' respective competitive advantages to promote private-sector growth and development, trade in goods and services, and direct foreign investment. The India-Japan Strategic and Global Partnership dates back to 2006, when PM Singh visited PM Abe in Tokyo during Abe's first term in office.

Other areas covered by the CEPA include nuclear power, renewable energy, energy efficiency, clean coal, climate change, and intellectual property. IP theft is a problem in India, but it is a criminal problem, not a state-sponsored assault on the most valuable technologies of foreign companies and governments. It does not appear to be a brake on the CEPA agenda. India and Japan are also cooperating to reduce China's influence on the market for rare-earth metals through the development of new sources, alternatives, and re-use.

Prime Minister Singh told the press that implementation of the CEPA would take place on a foundation of "democracy, rule of law, and respect for basic human freedoms" (*NetIndian*, October 25, 2010). This almost certainly means that progress will be slower than it would be in China, but it will also be more conducive to mutually satisfying long-term relationships. Japanese manufacturers see India as both a large new market and a low-cost production base.

At a meeting in Phnom Penh, Cambodia, in November 2012, the two countries' industry ministers reached agreement on a list of 19 infrastructure projects to be carried out in India with the support of Japan's Ministry of Economy, Trade, and Industry (METI); financial institutions; and private corporations. These involve electric power, railways, roads, ports, water systems, and urban development.

The flagship of Japan-India economic cooperation is the Delhi-Mumbai Industrial Corridor (DMIC) project, which includes a 1,483km (921-mile) freight railway linking the two cities, plus industrial parks, residential developments, and local transportation facilities along the way. Participants on the Japanese side include METI, the Japan International Cooperation Agency, the New Energy and Industrial Technology Development Organization, the City of Yokohama, Tokyo Electric Power, Tokyo Gas, general trading companies such as Mitsubishi Corp. and Itochu, major electrical equipment companies such as Hitachi and Toshiba, JGC and other engineering companies, NEC, Kyocera, and several other firms. The government-funded Japan Bank for International Cooperation owns 26% of DMIC.

Challenges facing the Japanese (and everyone else) in India include bureaucratic inertia, popular resistance, and theft of intellectual property. Bureaucratic inertia is a given, but the Japanese themselves are not known for rushing into things without meticulous consideration. But the Japanese are also known for doing things right and getting things done, so the end result, however long it might take to realize, is likely to be a major upgrade of infrastructure that in many cases is left over from the British Empire.

Popular resistance to economic development plans, and worker unrest, may lead to violence in India, as was the case at the Maruti Suzuki auto factory in Manesar in July 2012, when riots resulted in the death of a factory manager and dozens injured. More than 150 people were arrested and some 500 employees let go, but Suzuki did not abandon the joint venture, which is now 30 years old. The workforce and production volumes have since been rebuilt.

Suzuki Motor CEO Osamu Suzuki told the press, "We have no intention of leaving just because the incident occurred," adding that "India is our second home, after Japan" and announcing plans to expand production of subcompacts and other vehicles (*Nikkei*, September 4, 2013).

Other Japanese vehicle makers, including Honda, Toyota, Nissan, Isuzu, and Yamaha, are also expanding or planning to establish assembly operations in India. These are concentrated around the cities of Chennai and Bangalore in the state of Tamil Nadu, where European and American automakers also have assembly plants. More than 1,000 Japanese companies are now operating in India as a whole, with over 300 in Tamil Nadu, where the Japanese government is supporting improvements to land transportation, port facilities, and the power grid, which have not kept up with industrial development.

In February 2012, Toshiba JSW (a 75:25 joint venture between Toshiba and India's JSW Group) inaugurated its super-critical steam turbine and generator manufacturing plant in Chennai. The plant produces high-efficiency steam turbines and generators for thermal power plants with generating capacities ranging from 500MW to 1GW. It is intended to be Toshiba's second major production base for thermal power–generating equipment, complementing its domestic facilities and serving markets in India, Southeast Asia, and the Middle East. Targeted production capacity is 6GW per annum by 2015.

Toshiba CEO Norio Sasaki called the Chennai facility "essential to sustain the long-term growth of our global thermal power plant system business." Chairman Sajjan Jindal of JSW Energy said, "Establishing a state-of-art power equipment manufacturing facility in India is in line with our long term vision to present in the entire value chain of power business from equipment manufacturing, generation, transmission, power trading and distribution" (Toshiba press release, February 12, 2012). In addition to power-plant equipment, Toshiba's plans for India include streetcars powered by lithium-ion batteries, electronic road-toll collection systems, light rail, and other infrastructure and electronics.

Toshiba's largest Japanese competitors – Hitachi and Mitsubishi Heavy Industries (MHI) – also plan to develop India as an important market and production base. MHI has established a joint-venture steam turbine plant with Larsen & Toubro and is planning to build a gas-fired power plant with the Tata Group. Hitachi plans to begin production of steam turbines in India in 2014, has recently started production of inverters and uninterruptible power supplies, and is considering making railcar parts and railway signal equipment there as well.

Panasonic is also committed to India, having bought Anchor Electricals in 2007. Headquartered in Mumbai, Anchor makes some hundreds of millions of plugs, switches, and other electrical components per year. Panasonic is one of Japan's leading suppliers of housing fixtures, and the Indian housing market is more than five times larger than Japan's. The goal is a Japan-India manufacturing alliance that can compete effectively with China and South Korea, building economies of scale through the development of the Indian market while combining Japanese engineering expertise with relatively cheap Indian labor.

Prime Minister Abe's Quadrilateral Security Dialogue (QSD) between the United States, India, Japan, and Australia, launched in 2007, provided a framework for political-military ties between Japan and India. But the effort to create a bilateral strategic relationship goes back to former Japanese Prime Minister Yoshiro Mori's visit to India in 2000, when a "Global Partnership between Japan and India in the 21st Century" was announced. This has since evolved into the economic cooperation outlined above, frequent consultations on security issues, and naval exercises including the four Quadrilateral countries plus Singapore.

Abe's visit to New Delhi in 2007 took the process a step further: at a special session of the Indian Parliament, Mr. Abe called for an "arc of freedom and prosperity" along the rim of Asia. A dozen university vice-chancellors accompanied him in order to promote joint programs with Indian universities, underlining the longer-term importance of educational and people-to-people exchanges. Abe, who has a strong personal affinity for the country, returned to India in January 2014 accompanied by a large delegation of businessmen, and visited again in December 2015. The Emperor and Empress of Japan made a state visit to India in late 2013.

The election of Narendra Modi as India's new prime minister has taken Japan-India relations another step forward. Modi has a good personal relationship with Prime Minister Abe, who has said that Japan's ties with India have the "greatest potential of any bilateral relationship anywhere in the world" ("Narendra Modi: India's Shinzo Abe," *The Japan Times*, May 20, 2014).

Modi's five-day visit to Japan, starting on August 30, 2014, was a personal as well as a national affair. The Indian prime minister and Prime Minister Abe tweeted each other before the visit and shared a big hug at the airport and a visit to a Buddhist temple in Kyoto before summit meetings in Tokyo. The two leaders have gotten along very well for many years, and they are now in the position to take India-Japan economic and security relations to a new level.

The meetings themselves resulted in Japan announcing plans to double its total loans to, and investments in, India to 3.5 trillion yen (U.S.$33 billion) over the next five years, including a doubling of annual foreign direct investment by Japanese corporations to 400 billion yen ($3.8 billion), provided India simplifies and unifies its business regulations – replacing "red tape" with a "red carpet," as Modi put it in Tokyo. Most of Japan's government investments in India (including government-sponsored loans) have been, and will continue to be, for railways, roads, industrial zones, and other infrastructure.

While in Kyoto, Prime Minister Modi also met with Nidec CEO Shigenobu Nagamori. Nidec plans to invest about U.S.$1 billion in India over the next several years to build, or perhaps buy, factories to make motors for auto, consumer appliance, industrial, and other applications. Since his inauguration in May, Modi has also met with the top executives of Suzuki Motor, Mitsubishi Corp., and Fast Retailing (Uniqlo).

On the security side, India and Japan have agreed to hold regular joint exercises by the Japan Maritime Self-Defense Force and the Indian Navy, as well as further discussions regarding regular meetings between their foreign and defense ministers, three-way security discussions with the U.S., and the sale of Japanese amphibious search-and-rescue aircraft to India.

## Development Plan for Bangladesh

> **"Bangladesh has great economic potential. In order to realise its potential and expedite further growth, Japan has come up with the concept of the Bay of Bengal industrial growth belt."**
> – *Japanese Prime Minister Shinzo Abe, at a joint press conference with Bangladeshi Prime Minister Sheikh Hasina in Tokyo;*
> The Daily Star *(September 14, 2014)*

On September 6, 2014, Japanese Prime Minister Abe visited Bangladesh, where he discussed bilateral security cooperation, development aid, trade, and investment. The following week, Bangladeshi Prime Minister Sheikh Hasina was in Tokyo to continue discussions cementing the relationship. She also met with Japanese Emperor Akihito at the Imperial Palace.

Bangladesh has a population of more than 150 million and an economy that has recently been growing at an annual rate of about 6%. The world's second-largest exporter of textiles after China, its growth has been supported by cheap labor. Aiming to raise the share of manufacturing in the economy and move up the value chain, its government is now promoting the upgrade of port and water control facilities, roads, railways, bridges, power generation (including a second nuclear power plant), and other infrastructure.

Japan – which lags China, India, Singapore, Malaysia, and South Korea in exports to Bangladesh and competes with China in infrastructure investment – hopes to expand its presence in the country by continuing an already substantial Overseas Development Assistance (ODA) program and promoting the construction of the Bay of Bengal Industrial Growth Belt (BIG-B), running from Dhaka southeast along the Bay of Bengal toward Myanmar. Specifically, the Japanese government plans to extend ¥600 billion (USD $5.6 billion) worth of loans to Bangladesh over the next four to five years and hopes to create opportunities for the Japanese private sector.

Executives from about 20 major Japanese companies, including Mitsubishi Heavy Industries, IHI, and Shimizu Construction, accompanied Mr. Abe on his visit to Bangladesh. In return for Japanese economic support, Prime Minister Hasina agreed to support Japan's bid for a nonpermanent seat on the United Nations Security Council.

Abe's visit followed an agreement on the Japan-Bangladesh Comprehensive Partnership at the Japan-Bangladesh Summit Meeting in May 2014. The president of the Japan International Cooperation Agency visited Bangladesh in June to discuss five projects for which ODA agreements have already been signed, as well as future projects, including the BIG-B.

Japan is promoting – and even planning – the industrialization of a country that has a larger and younger population and a nominal per-capita GDP of about U.S.$1,200. For Japan (and other East Asian countries), Bangladesh has great potential as a buyer of infrastructure and capital goods, a growing consumer market, and a site for low-cost manufacturing. Honda, for example, is planning to build a new, larger motorcycle factory there, as consumer spending is reaching the take-off stage. The leading importers of goods from Bangladesh are the U.S., Germany, the United Kingdom, and France.

## Progress in Myanmar

**"If you think about our strengths in natural resources, energy and infrastructure, each of these sectors in Myanmar have significant opportunities."**
*– Andrew Géczy, Chief Executive for International and Institutional Banking, Australia & New Zealand Banking Group – the only non-Asian bank to be awarded a license in Myanmar* (The Wall Street Journal, *October 1, 2014*)

On October 1, 2014, the government of Myanmar granted licenses to nine foreign banks, including the Bank of Tokyo-Mitsubishi UFJ, Sumitomo Mitsui Banking Corp., and Mizuho Bank from Japan; UOB and OCBC Bank from Singapore; the Industrial and Commercial Bank from China (PRC); Bangkok Bank from Thailand; Maybank from Malaysia; and the Australia and New Zealand Banking Group (ANZ). Three South Korean, three Taiwanese, and one Indian bank also applied for – but failed to win – licenses. No American or European banks bothered to apply.

Three Japanese banks received licenses after lobbying by Prime Minster Abe and visits to Myanmar by their presidents. The Singaporean banks benefited from lobbying by Prime Minister Lee Hsien Loong. The South Koreans tried a similar strategy, but it didn't work, apparently due to the relatively small size and limited international experience of their banks. The Europeans and Americans were reportedly put off by the need to make long-term commitments to what could be a difficult process of modernization with little or no profit for several years. In addition, the U.S. government discouraged American participation, canceling some of its economic sanctions against Myanmar earlier in the year but extending others to protest what it regarded as insufficient democratization.

In addition to running banks, the Japanese are taking measures to promote economic development and the activities of their private sector in Myanmar. So far, such assistance has included the cancellation of old debts and the financing of infrastructure, manufacturing, and service businesses.

In October, Japanese trading company Marubeni, in a consortium with Thai utilities, was chosen to build an ultra-super-critical coal-fired power plant in Myanmar, which will both relieve local power shortages and export power to Thailand. Ultra-super-critical coal-burning technology, which is advertised as being 20% more efficient than conventional technology, is a specialty of the Japanese heavy industrial companies that are likely to supply the equipment.

Also in October 2014, a consortium led by Yongnam Holdings of Singapore and including Singapore's Changi Airport Planners and Engineers and Japanese engineering company JGC won the contract to design and build Myanmar's new international airport after a deal with South Korea fell through.

Panasonic plans to establish product showrooms, a sales training program, and maintenance services in Myanmar, hoping to catch up with South Korean and Chinese rivals by tripling sales of air conditioners, refrigerators, TVs, solar panels, storage batteries, and other products by 2018.

Japanese trading company Sumitomo Corp. and telecom carrier KDDI plan to invest U.S.$2 billion in Myanmar Posts & Telecommunications (MPT) over the next 10 years in an attempt to maintain the lead their joint ventures enjoy in the country's mobile communications market.

State-owned MPT had a monopoly until mid-2013. The joint venture with Sumitomo and KDDI, formed as part of the government's market liberalization and technology upgrade program, faces competition from Ooredoo of Qatar and Telenor of Norway, which were licensed in 2013.

In November, U.S. President Barack Obama visited Myanmar

to lend support to opposition leader Aung San Suu Kyi and the country's democratic reforms. He did not bring any corporate executives with him and did not offer any economic assistance. *Bloomberg Businessweek* stated that Obama was visiting "a country where optimism…has dimmed to black…so disastrous that most U.S. investors…are giving Myanmar a wide berth." Or simply missing the boat. The Coca-Cola Co. established a bottling plant in Myanmar in 2013, and KFC, in partnership with Yoma Strategic Holdings of Singapore, is planning to open its first franchise there in 2015. *BBC News* reported in mid-October 2014 that KFC calls Myanmar "an important emerging Asian economy with a population of 50 million people."

Recently, Myanmar has announced plans to allow foreign insurance companies to operate outside special economic zones. Myanmar's deputy finance minister told the press: "Three of the Japanese top insurance companies have been having representative office in Myanmar for more than 17 years. Other foreign companies have rep office for one year or two year[s]. We have to acknowledge the patience, the perseverance and the loyalty of insurance companies who have such qualities" (*Nikkei*, January 23, 2015).

The *Nikkei* also reports that JFE Engineering, an affiliate of one of Japan's largest steelmakers, is training women engineering students from Myanmar in Japan. JFE Engineering is building bridges and other infrastructure in Myanmar through a joint venture with Myanmar's Ministry of Construction.

## Partnership with Turkey

Turkey is on a campaign to diversify its trade and sources of foreign investment away from the European Union, and Japan is building an economic partnership with Turkey, as are China and South Korea. The share of Turkish exports going to the EU dropped from 58% in 2003 to 39% in 2013, while the share going to the Middle East rose from 11%

to 28%, and the share going to Asia-Pacific rose from 2% to 7%. Trade with China increased by more than eight times during the same period.

Given the size of the East Asia economies, that is where the greatest potential for further growth lies, and that is where the Turkish government is focusing its efforts. A free-trade agreement (FTA) with South Korea took effect in May 2013, and FTA and / or economic-partnership agreements (EPA) are being discussed with India, Thailand, Malaysia, Singapore, Indonesia, and Japan. Turkey / Japan trade is still low, at about U.S.$4 billion per year, and Japanese investment in Turkey amounts to only $1.5 billion. EPA negotiations between the two are aimed at providing a framework for a substantial increase in these figures.

The Turkish government is also looking to East Asia for investment, technology, and participation in infrastructure projects, so far with great success. Test runs on the Ankara-Istanbul high-speed railway, built by China Railway Construction Corp., began in January 2014. In October 2013, Prime Minister Abe attended the opening ceremony for the Bosphorus Strait Railway Tunnel, which was built by Japanese general contractor Taisei. Japanese engineering company IHI is building what will be the world's fourth-longest suspension bridge across Izmit Bay on the new highway between Istanbul and Izmir and renovating the first and second Bosphorus bridges, which it built 40 and 25 years ago, respectively.

On the industrial side, Mitsubishi Heavy Industries and the trading company Itochu of Japan and Areva and GDF Suez of France have been chosen to build Turkey's second nuclear power plant. (Rosatom and ZAO Atomstroyexport of Russia were selected to build the first.) In 2011, Mitsubishi Electric won an order to supply Turkey with two communications satellites, in part due its willingness to transfer technology, which Alcatel and Lockheed Martin were reportedly reluctant to do. TURKSAT-4A was launched from the Baikonur Cosmodrome in February 2014; TURKSAT-4B is scheduled to be launched in 2015.

## Advantage Africa

**"Japan will not simply bring natural resources from Africa to Japan. We want to realise industrialisation in Africa that will generate employment and growth."**
*– Japanese Prime Minister Shinzo Abe, June 3, 2013*

The 5th Tokyo International Conference on African Development (TICAD V), held in June 2013, attracted delegates from 51 African countries, including 39 heads of state. Prime Minister Abe told them that "in the next five years, we will support Africa's economic development by providing up to $32 billion in public and private funding" (*The Wall Street Journal*, June 2, 2013) – a figure that would likely match or exceed China's assistance over the same period .

The plan and the interests of target countries including Kenya, Mozambique, and Tunisia encompass infrastructure, private sector investment, environmental technology, training for 30,000 local personnel, and academic exchange. Sectors targeted for investment include oil, gas, coal, and the mining of platinum and other metals; ports and harbors; and power generation auto assembly, among other manufacturing.

In July 2013, immediately after TICAD V, Kansai Paint – one of Japan's two largest paint manufacturers – announced plans to purchase 62.5% of Astra Industries from the Finance Trust of Zimbabwe. Astra is Zimbabwe's largest paint maker, with about 40% of the market. Kansai Paint's South African subsidiary Kansai Plascon Africa already has factories in Botswana, Namibia, Zambia, and Malawi, and exports to Mozambique, the Seychelles, Mauritius, Kenya, Nigeria, and other countries. Substantial investments in South Africa have been made by Nissan and Toyota (vehicle assembly) and Bridgestone (tires). According to Japanese government data, more than 110 Japanese companies are currently operating In South Africa alone, generating approximately 150,000 jobs.

Data from the Japan External Trade Organization shows Japanese direct investment in and trade with Africa to be less than 20% of China's. The Abe government hopes to greatly increase investment and triple Japanese exports to Africa by 2020. World Bank president Jim Yong Kim told Japanese finance minister and deputy prime minister Taro Aso that the World Bank would help Japanese companies expand in Africa.

These efforts should add further impetus to African economic growth and give African governments and companies more bargaining power in their dealings with foreign governments and corporations. Unlike the Chinese, the Japanese have no surplus of low-paid workers that they can bring with them to fill the jobs they create in Africa. Considering the rapid development of African economies and the need to create more skilled jobs, the timing appears to be very good.

Japan's Cumulative Foreign Direct
Investment in Africa 2002–2013 (USD billions)

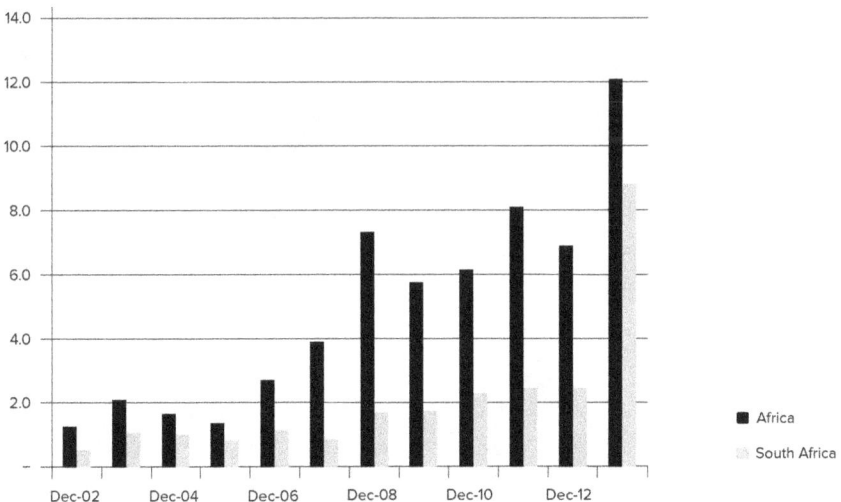

Sources: JETRO, Japan Ministry of Finance

## Japan's Trade with Africa 2002–2013 (USD billions)

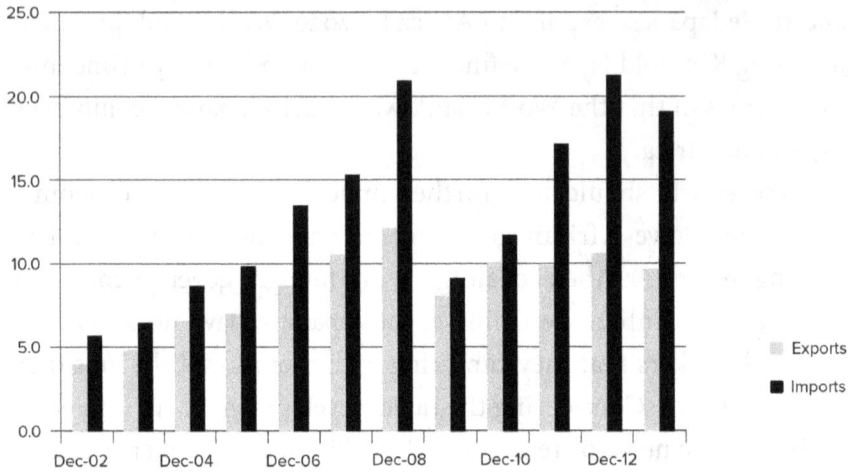

Source: WTO

# V.

# Taking the InfoMercantilist Model into the Next Century

Abenomics or no Abenomics, the Japanese are pursuing several initiatives that may have a significant long-term economic impact, including:

- Hydrogen-based energy systems
- Seabed mining
- "Eco-cities"
- Advanced aircraft manufacturing
- Deregulation of military equipment exports
- Overseas nuclear power plant projects

In addition, Japan and the Asian Development Bank (ADB) are launching a new fund to promote the construction of environmentally friendly infrastructure – including wind and geothermal power, waste-to-energy power systems, and smart grids – "in Indonesia, Vietnam, Bangladesh, Cambodia, and other Asian countries that have agreed to adopt a carbon credit exchange system with Japan" (*Nikkei*, April 21, 2014). The ADB is traditionally headed by a Japanese national. Its current president, Takehiko Nakao, who was previously a senior official in the Ministry of Finance, succeeded

Haruhiko Kuroda, who resigned from the ADB in March 2013 to head the Bank of Japan.

The Japanese government is working with Japanese banks, trading companies, and industrial equipment manufacturers to replace old and dirty coal-fired power plants with cleaner-burning super-critical coal-fired power plants, in Southeast Asia and elsewhere. It's also introducing circulating fluidized bed boilers that can burn low-grade coal, waste from palm-oil plantations, and other biomass.

Japanese engineering companies are playing a key role in the conversion of the world's energy systems from oil and coal to gas. JGC and Chiyoda, which together have designed more than 60% of the world's liquefied natural gas (LNG) facilities, are forming joint ventures with Fluor, Technip, and other engineering companies to bid for projects in North America, Asia-Pacific, the Middle East, Africa, and Russia.

In April 2013, JGC and Technip were awarded the engineering, procurement, and construction (EPC) contract for Novatek and Total's Yamal LNG project on the Arctic coast of Russia. In January 2014, JGC and Fluor won the EPC contract for Chevron and Apache Canada's Kitimat LNG project at Bish Cove, British Columbia. In April 2014, a Chiyoda-led consortium including Foster-Wheeler, Saipem, and WorleyParsons were selected to build the liquefaction terminal at Royal Dutch Shell's LNG Canada project, also located in Kitimat. Shell's minority investment partners include PetroChina, Korea Gas, and Mitsubishi Corp.

## Hydrogen Infrastructure

Japan has what is probably the most advanced and most diverse hydrogen energy development program in the world. In mid-December 2014, Toyota launched its first hydrogen fuel-cell vehicle (FCV) for the passenger-car market: the Mirai (*mirai* means "future"), a four-seater sedan. Priced at ¥5.2 million (roughly U.S.$43,000) after a government subsidy, it is already sold out, and annual production capacity will be tripled to 2,100 units per year to meet initial demand. The Mirai is scheduled to be launched in the U.S. and Europe in late 2015. Honda is also expected to launch its own mass-market FCV within the next several months.

Tokyo Gas opened Japan's first commercial hydrogen fueling station three days after the Mirai launch; and JX Nippon Oil & Energy, which operates the Eneos chain of gasoline stations, started to build its own network in January 2015. The government of Tokyo aims to establish 80 hydrogen stations in partnership with the private sector, while JX plans to establish about 2,000 stations nationwide, supplied from 10 hydrogen production facilities. Toyota has designed trailer-type hydrogen fueling stations that resemble gasoline stands, which can be moved from place to place; the mobile stations will be smaller and cheaper. Several other companies are also getting involved.

In the U.S., Toyota has loaned $7.3 million to FirstElement Fuel to help it build hydrogen fueling stations in California. FirstElement, which received a $27.6 million grant from the California Energy Commission at the beginning of May 2014, plans to build 19 stations around the state. Toyota estimates that 68 will be required to serve 10,000 fuel-cell vehicles to ensure that they don't get stranded. It expects 50 to be built by the end of 2016 and hopes to have 70 in operation a year later. Initially, the stations will be supplied by truck. Stations that generate hydrogen onsite are expected to follow once costs come down.

Meanwhile, Chiyoda Corp. – one of Japan's top engineering companies – has developed what it calls a "large-scale hydrogen storage and transportation system," in which hydrogen gas is fixed to toluene. The resulting compound, methylcyclohexane, can then be transported by ship or truck and kept in storage tanks in liquid form. When the reaction is reversed, the hydrogen gas is released.

Chiyoda is working with the City of Kawasaki on plans for the use of hydrogen fuel in the Keihin Industrial Zone on the west side of Tokyo Bay. The technology may also be used to transport hydrogen to FCV fueling stations as part of Japan's Hydrogen & Fuel Cell Project. JX has announced plans to deliver hydrogen dissolved in toluene to its own network of fueling stations starting in 2020.

In addition, Nippon Steel & Sumitomo Metal Corp. is building an experimental hydrogen-fueled blast furnace at its Kimitsu steelworks on the east side of Tokyo Bay. This follows several years of research by the Japan Iron and Steel Federation and Japan's New Energy and Industrial Technology Development Organization. As reported by the *Nikkei* (August 7, 2013), "the aim [of the project] is to slash industry $CO_2$ emissions by 30% by 2030, with 10% coming from a partial changeover from coal to hydrogen. While just four companies use blast furnaces [in Japan], they account for 15% of the nation's total $CO_2$ emissions." Hydrogen is a byproduct of traditional steelmaking.

In Fukuoka Prefecture, on the north end of the island of Kyushu, the Kitakyushu Smart Community Project is connecting Honda-made hydrogen FCVs to homes and offices in an energy management system. The fuel cells are powered by hydrogen sent by pipeline from Nippon Steel & Sumitomo Metal Corp.'s Yawata plant, which is located nearby. There are four similar projects elsewhere in Japan supported by steel, oil, auto, and electric machinery companies.

## Seabed Mining

In 2011, Japanese scientists announced the discovery of high concentrations of rare-earth elements and yttrium in seafloor sediments in the vicinity of Hawaii and Tahiti. The deposits, at depths of 3,500 to 6,000 meters and covering some 11 million square meters in international waters, may exceed deposits on land by 1,000 times. To quote from their report:

> We estimate that an area of just one square kilometre, surrounding one of the sampling sites, could provide one-fifth of the current annual world consumption of these elements. Uptake of rare-earth elements and yttrium by mineral phases such as hydrothermal iron-oxyhydroxides and phillipsite seems to be responsible for their high concentration. We show that rare-earth elements and yttrium are readily recovered from the mud by simple acid leaching, and suggest that deep-sea mud constitutes a highly promising huge resource for these elements.
>
> – *Assistant Professor Kato Yasuhiro , University of Tokyo*
> (Nature Geoscience, *July 3, 2011)*

In March 2013, a team of scientists from the Japan Agency for Marine-Earth Science and Technology (JAMSTEC) and the University of Tokyo announced that they had found a deposit of the rare-earth element dysprosium under the seabed in waters more than 5,000 meters deep near Minami-Torishima, a Japanese island nearly 2,000km (1,240 miles) southeast of Tokyo. Dysprosium is used in laser materials, lighting, dosimeters, and motors for hybrid vehicles, among other applications. With concentrations up to 32 times greater than those found in China, the deposit is estimated to contain a 230-year supply of the element. Japan's METI plans to survey the area and drill in some 40 locations by 2016.

JAMSTEC operates the *Chikyu* – the world's largest deep-sea drilling vessel and the primary research vessel of the multinational

Integrated Ocean Drilling Program (which includes Japan, China, the U.S., and European nations). It has also developed an undersea robot with a new drive mechanism designed for negotiating sandy, rocky, and steep surfaces while searching for and collecting mineral samples on the sea floor. These and other sub-sea vessels are built by Mitsui Engineering & Shipbuilding and other Japanese engineering companies.

In March 2013, a research team from the Japan Oil, Gas, and Metals National Corp. (JOGMEC) working on the *Chikyu* announced that it had "extracted natural gas from a deposit of methane hydrate under the seabed off the coasts of Aichi and Mie prefectures [west of Tokyo]. Methane hydrate deposits under the waters off Aichi and Mie are estimated to be equal [to] 10 years' worth of domestic natural gas consumption" (*Nikkei,* March 11 and 12, 2013).

JOGMEC plans to develop methane hydrate production technology before 2020. Many other nations are attempting to turn methane hydrate deposits into a commercial energy source, but Japan has reportedly outspent all of them – including the United States, China, Russia, and Germany. Estimates of the potential range from being too environmentally dangerous to pursue, due to the possibility of greenhouse gas leakage and tsunami-generating underwater mudslides, to a century's worth of natural gas.

## The Seas of Japan

Japan's territorial waters and Exclusive Economic Zone are about 12 times larger than its land area, and the sixth-largest in the world.

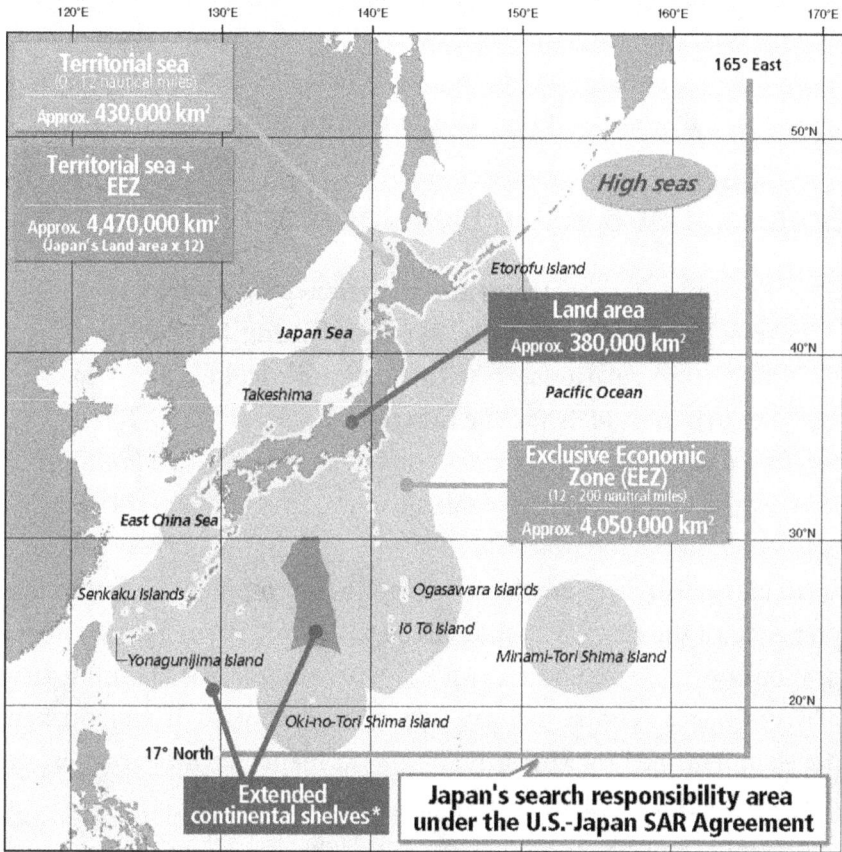

Source: Japan Coast Guard

[SAR = Search and Rescue]

The area around Etorofu and the other southern Kuril Islands northeast of Hokkaido is claimed by Japan but administered as part of Russia's Sakhalin Oblast. Takeshima, located in the Japan Sea, is claimed by Japan but occupied and controlled by South Korea. The Senkaku Islands, located in the far southwest corner of Japan's territorial waters, are controlled by Japan but claimed by China.

Before the discovery of resources at the bottom of the sea and the development of the equipment needed to extract them, dependence on imported energy and minerals caused the Japanese to regard their home as a narrow (small) country, poor in natural resources. Given its excellent farmland and abundant water, this was never precisely true; but in the future, it may make no sense at all.

## Smart Cities & Asian Development

"Portland demonstrates a true balance of smart urban growth and affordability. We are looking forward to a long-term relationship with Portland's leaders in creating urban models for the future."
– *Yasuo Onozawa, President and CEO, Smart City Planning Inc.*
(Sustainable Business Oregon, *January 23, 2014*)

In January 2014, the Portland (Oregon) Development Commission, on behalf of the city's We Build Green Cities initiative, signed a Memorandum of Understanding (MOU) with Smart City Planning Inc., a Tokyo-based venture dedicated to environmentally friendly urban development. Led by Mitsui Fudosan – a major Japanese real-estate developer – Smart City Planning is a consortium of 25 Japanese companies plus South Korea's LG CNS and Hewlett-Packard.

Under the MOU, a team of We Build Green Cities companies led by ZGF Architects has entered into a contract with Mitsui Fudosan to provide planning and design services for an energy management system in Kashiwa-no-ha Campus City, a smart-city project northeast of Tokyo. (*Disclosure:* The author has a relative who is a partner at ZGF.) The plan is to build an energy-efficient, low-carbon academic city and entrepreneurial center focused on healthcare and agriculture 30 minutes from downtown Tokyo and two Tsukuba Express stops away from Tsukuba Science City.

Of several other smart-city projects underway in Japan, the largest and most prominent is in Yokohama, with others in Toyota City, Kyoto, Kitakyushu, and elsewhere. The Yokohama Smart City Project grew out of the need to modernize the city's housing and water, electric power, and transport infrastructure. The Yokohama Partnership of Resources and Technologies (Y-PORT) works with local and other Japanese companies on urban renewal projects in India, Indonesia, Vietnam, the Philippines, and other countries in Asia.

Every year, a Smart City Week exhibition and Asia Smart City Conference are held in Yokohama. The exhibition features the products and displays of private companies, as well as industrial, governmental, and academic institutions from Japan and around the world. Japanese electronics and engineering conglomerates – including Toshiba, Hitachi, and Mitsubishi Electric – are using the event to develop integrated markets for home, commercial building, factory, and community energy management; and for water, transport, logistics, and IT systems.

In 2014, participants in the Asia Smart City Conference – which is supported by Japan's Ministry of Foreign Affairs, the Ministry of the Environment, and the Japan International Cooperation Agency – included 22 Asian cities, plus the Asian Development Bank, the World Resource Institute, and the C40 Cities Climate Leadership Group.

Japan's METI sees smart cities as a way to help Japanese corporations develop new markets overseas. It defines a "smart community" as "a new concept of urban development with a...combination of smart grids, renewable energy, urban transportation, water treatment, recycling, information and communication technology, and other environmental and system technology where Japan has an advantage." In a publication entitled "Launching International Feasibility Studies on the 'Smart Community' Concept," METI notes that:

> Strong promotion of overseas development of infrastructure and systems through public-private cooperation will enable Japan to contribute to environmental issues in Asia

and other emerging countries during their rapid growth, and further, throughout the world in general. At the same time, it is an extremely important approach in Japan's industrial strategy.

The Nikkei BP Cleantech Institute has a more limited definition of the smart-city market, which includes smart grids; solar, wind, and other renewable energy; storage batteries; next-generation vehicles; EV chargers; and IT systems – but not water, waste disposal, roads, railways, airports, or other basic infrastructure. It estimates that smart-city–related demand will grow from being hardly worth mentioning in 2010 to a cumulative total of more than U.S. $40 trillion by 2030. Based on a study of 100 smart-city projects (out of more than 300 worldwide), Nikkei BP forecasts that America, Europe, China, and Asia ex-China will each account for about 20% of the total value.

The Japanese are also participating in Singapore-led smart-city projects in Tianjin and Guangzhou. Sino-Singapore Tianjin Eco-City is the second joint urban development project conducted by the governments of Singapore and China (the Suzhou Industrial Park being the first). Beginning with a framework agreement in 2007, it aims to build a Singapore-like city of 350,000 people by 2020. The goal is to create a city that is commercially viable, affordable, compact, and environmentally sustainable. It would have business parks and services located near residential areas to shorten commutes (land-use planning), with an emphasis on public transport, bicycles, walking, and the separation of motorized and non-motorized traffic (transport planning). Parks, other greenery, and bodies of water in and around the city (green and blue network planning) would enhance the environment.

According to the International Enterprise (IE) Singapore website, the Tianjin Eco-city project is aimed at "supporting the overseas growth of Singapore-based companies." But it is not exclusive.

Japanese electrical and industrial conglomerate Hitachi is developing the city's smart grid, home energy systems, EV charging systems, and other environmentally friendly urban infrastructure. It is also participating in a Sino-Singapore Guangzhou Knowledge City, where it plans to establish a Smart City R&D center.

Unfortunately, all this effort is being suffocated by the world-leading air pollution created by the Chinese government's historical emphasis on economic growth. Chinese air pollution – now darkening the sky in Seoul, a problem in Japan, and measurable even in Portland, Oregon – has gotten to the point where smog can be seen and masks should be worn inside China's new high-speed railway cars when traveling through the countryside. In the cities, it is making life almost unbearable.

With time, the smart-city concept is likely to spread all over Asia, creating large opportunities for private design and engineering firms in the context of government and public-private planning. Fortunately, the American example attracting attention in Asia is Portland, not Detroit.

## Lessons for Boeing & Mitsubishi

In October 2013, Japan Airlines (JAL) ordered 31 Airbus A350 aircraft, ending a single-supplier relationship with Boeing that had lasted for six decades. There were two reasons given for the change: delays and technical problems with the Boeing 787 and the bankruptcy of JAL. JAL's bankruptcy had various causes, including high operating costs, over-expansion, excessive borrowing, and paying too much for aircraft. There was an "understanding" that Japanese airlines would buy aircraft from Boeing, and Boeing would outsource parts manufacturing to Japan.

Kazuo Inamori, founder of electronics manufacturer Kyocera and telecom service provider KDDI, became chairman and CEO of

JAL in 2010 at the request of then–Prime Minister Yukio Hatoyama. Three years later, JAL was once again profitable, relisted on the Tokyo Stock Exchange and governed by normal business practices. "In a normal market there is tremendous risk from relying on one vendor," said Mr. Inamori. "[To encourage competitive pricing and quality] a dual vendor system is a must" (*Nikkei*, Oct. 15, 2013).

Prior to the Airbus order, Boeing supplied 100% of the large passenger jets flown by JAL and more than 90% of those flown by All Nippon Airways (ANA). How much of the market Airbus can take in Japan remains unclear, but in March 2014, ANA announced plans to buy 40 new aircraft from Boeing and 30 from Airbus between 2016 and 2027. At present, only 44 Airbus aircraft are flown by Japanese airlines, most of them smaller models on local routes. By comparison, JAL and ANA together fly more than 300 Boeing aircraft.

According to industry sources, about 35% of the Boeing 787 is made in Japan, including wing and fuselage assemblies from Mitsubishi Heavy Industries (MHI) and Kawasaki Heavy Industries (KHI), carbon fiber from Toray, and other components. This has led some commentators to forecast disaster for MHI and other Japanese makers of aircraft parts as the other side of the "understanding" is unwound.

In the end, the issue comes down to supply-chain management – and not only for Boeing. In August 2013, MHI announced the third delay to its Mitsubishi Regional Jet (MRJ) project, which aims to develop 70- to 90-seat passenger aircraft for middle-distance routes in Asia and elsewhere. The first delivery of MRJ aircraft has now been pushed out to mid-2017, two years later than originally planned. "Supplier management is no easy task," an MHI manager told the press. "Our expertise in this area is next to nothing" (*Nikkei*, September 2, 2013).

Final assembly of the first flight-test MRJ aircraft began in October 2013. The engines are made by Pratt & Whitney. Boeing will handle spare parts provisioning and other customer support services. So far, ANA, JAL, and three American customers have ordered more than 400 MRJ aircraft (including options), which in management's estimation should get the project to break-even.

Airbus is now expanding its Japanese supplier network, which currently provides fewer than 10% of the parts used in its aircraft. Japanese companies in its supply chain include KHI (engine parts), Toray and Teijin (carbon fiber), and Sumitomo Precision (landing gear).

Meanwhile, Boeing, several of its Japanese suppliers (including MHI), and related makers of metalworking equipment, in cooperation with the Institute of Industrial Science at the University of Tokyo and METI, have established the Collaborative Research Center for Manufacturing Innovation (CMI). CMI aims to reduce aircraft production costs by 50% and shorten delivery times by 20%–50%.

In short, Boeing's ties with its Japanese suppliers are deepening, not disappearing, and Japanese aircraft parts makers are developing new business with Airbus. And while the news media write about the threat from China's attempts to build commercial aircraft, a new Japanese competitor is emerging from under the wing of Boeing.

## HondaJet

Honda is entering the market for business and personal jet aircraft. At the end of June 2014, the first HondaJet produced for shipment to a customer made its initial test flight at Piedmont Triad International Airport near Greensboro, North Carolina. Honda Aircraft's world headquarters and factory are located next to the airport. If all goes according to plan, FAA type certification should be received and deliveries should begin in the first half of 2015. A distribution and service network is already in place in North America and Europe.

The HondaJet is a five-passenger aircraft powered by two GE Honda HF115 Turbofan jet engines, with a maximum cruise speed of 420 knots (483 miles) per hour, a 1,611-mile range, and a maximum operating limit of 43,000 feet. Honda Aircraft claims that its patented over-the-wing engine mount (unique in a world of common designs), laminar flow wings, and composite fuselage make the HondaJet the "fastest, highest-flying, quietest, and most fuel-efficient jet in its class." Obviously, it does not yet have a track record, but given the history of Honda Motor, competitors have cause for concern.

Honda began flight tests of an experimental business jet in 2003. Honda Aircraft Co., a 100%-owned subsidiary of Honda Motor, was established in 2006. President and CEO Michimasa Fujino – who as chief engineer led the development of HondaJet – had spent the previous 20 years in aviation-related activities at Honda R&D Co. The first flight of an FAA-conforming Honda-Jet was made in December 2010. Commercial production began in October 2013. Deliveries should start as soon as type certification is received.

Soichiro Honda, the founder of Honda Motor, had always wanted to build airplanes. He and his wife had private-pilot's licenses, and he continued hang-gliding and ballooning into his 70s. A lifelong mechanic with no formal education, he was famous for his oil-stained hands, his pink suits, and his determination. In 1963, MITI proposed a Specified Industry Promotion Law to limit the number of Japanese companies allowed to make passenger cars in a way that would have excluded Honda Motor. In a 1983 interview on NHK television, Mr. Honda described an encounter with a senior MITI official as follows:

I deluged him with complaints, because I couldn't understand it at all. To hell with the Specified Industry Promotion Law! I had the right to manufacture automobiles, and they couldn't enforce a law that would allow only the existing manufacturers to build them while preventing us from doing the same. We were free to do exactly what we wanted. Besides, no one could say for certain that those in power would remain there forever. Look at history.... Eventually, a new power would always arise. I shouted at him angrily, saying that if MITI wanted us to merge (form a joint venture with another company), then they should buy our shares and propose it at our shareholders' meeting. After all, we were a public company. The government couldn't tell me what to do.

## Deregulating Arms Exports

On April 1, 2014, the Japanese government announced new rules governing exports of weapons and other military equipment, reversing a comprehensive ban on such exports adopted in 1967 and strengthened in 1976.

Whereas the old policy had been subject to special exceptions (e.g., the development of a joint missile-defense system with the U.S.), the new policy lays out clear guidelines for exports and technological cooperation, requiring detailed reviews to determine if such activities would contribute to national security or international peace. It is aimed at strengthening ties with allies and strategic partners, including the United States, Australia, the Philippines, Vietnam, India,

France, and the United Kingdom. Final decisions will be made by Japan's new National Security Council, which was established by the Abe administration in December 2013.

The new policy should contribute to the technological advance and economic viability of Japan's defense industry by allowing joint development and production of weapons systems and related equipment and by increasing the size of the potential market. Exports already in the pipeline or under discussion include ships and aircraft for surveillance, transport, rescue and minesweeping, submarine technology (to Australia), sensors used in surface-to-air missiles, and other components. Japanese companies will also make parts for the F-35 fighter jet. Joint development of weapons systems with the United States, Great Britain, France, and Australia is already accelerating.

MHI, KHI, Mitsubishi Electric, Sumitomo Precision, and other Japanese defense contractors have heretofore been confined to a domestic market that makes up only 4% of worldwide military-related sales. They now have an opportunity to develop much greater economies of scale – and to compete with South Korea, which is aggressively expanding its own arms exports. The U.S., seeking to strengthen its key alliance in the western Pacific, is an enthusiastic supporter of the change. How enthusiastic will it be if the Japanese defense industry, like the Japanese auto industry, turns into a major competitor? Perhaps, as was the case with the U.S. auto industry 50 years ago, it is concentrating on more immediate concerns.

Japan has one of the world's largest and most sophisticated military forces, which its defense industry supplies with everything from bullets to vertical take-off and landing aircraft carriers. Working within the constraints of a pacifist constitution, Japan has also developed a wide range of dual-use equipment technologies. These include the ships and aircraft mentioned above, which can be used for disaster relief; high-resolution satellite surveillance systems, which can be used for geographical surveys related to economic development; satellite communications; and rocket propulsion and guidance systems.

Japan's first export of Earth observation satellites was to Vietnam in 2011. It was financed "through overseas development assistance loans...as part of a broader 92.6 billion yen ($1.2 billion) package that includes the building of a major shipping port, a highway project and efforts to bolster flood-prone Vietnam's ability to respond to natural disasters" ("Japan, Vietnam Sign Deal for Two Radar Imaging Satellites," *SpaceNews*, November 4, 2011). This, of course, is of direct relevance to China's activities in the South China Sea.

## Fukushima

> **"Risks posed by the heavily contaminated water at the Fukushima Daiichi nuclear power plant will be minimal in about seven years if the current water-processing equipment operates as planned."**
> – *Conclusion of a Japanese government expert panel*
> (Nikkei, *December 4, 2013*)

Just as the Japanese Olympic Team entered the stadium at the opening ceremony of the Winter Olympics in Sochi in February 2014, a message appeared on television screens in Japan: *Earthquake in Fukushima, No tsunami expected.* There were several more small earthquakes off the coast of Fukushima in 2014 – none big enough to cause serious damage, but all reminders of a problem that won't be going away anytime soon.

Public-opinion polls in Japan consistently show a majority of respondents in favor of abandoning nuclear power altogether, but gradually, in a managed process that takes into account the nation's financial difficulties (electric power companies near bankruptcy, large national debt), trade and current account deficits caused by fossil-fuel imports, and the small contribution of renewables to the energy mix (an estimated 12%-13%, of which about 9% is hydroelectric). Elections for the National Diet, the Tokyo assembly, and, most recently, the governor of Tokyo have been a letdown for single-issue anti-nuclear candidates.

In February 2014, Tokyo voters gave Yoichi Masuzoe – a former health minister who supports Prime Minster Abe's plan to restart nuclear reactors – 2.1 million votes. Kenji Utsunomiya – a lawyer backed by the Communist Party who campaigned on a broad platform of social issues as well as opposition to nuclear power – and former Prime Minister Morihiro Hosokawa, who aimed to turn the governorship into a platform to oppose nuclear power nationwide, received just under 1 million votes each. General Toshio Tamogami, former chief of staff of the Air Force and prominent right-wing nationalist, received just over 600,000 votes. Polls showed nuclear and other energy issues ranking third in importance in the minds of voters, after health & welfare and the economy & employment.

Meanwhile, all of Japan's 54 nuclear power plants are still shut down for inspections and surveys by geologists to determine whether or not there are any active faults nearby. This is a useful exercise, but the fact remains that the entire Japanese archipelago can be regarded as an active fault zone. Nevertheless, if nuclear power plants are not turned back on, Japanese consumers, who have already seen their electric power rates go up about 15%, could lose even more of their disposable income; electric power companies could require a hugely expensive bail-out; and Prime Minister Abe's financial and economic revitalization policies may fail.

In February 2014, a draft of the Japanese government's new Basic Energy Plan was made public. It refers to nuclear power as an "important base-load electricity source" and does not include the previous plan's commitment to eliminate nuclear power completely over time. Following the completion of safety inspections, the restart of one or two reactors is likely to take place in 2015.

# Faith in Technology

Shortly after the Great East Japan Earthquake and Fukushima nuclear disaster of March 2011, I received a message from a university professor in Canada asking if the Japanese could ever get over the shock and if their faith in technology could survive. Four years later, the answers are "Yes" and "Yes," and the questions themselves seem irrelevant. The more important issue was always whether Japan could shake off its economic, political, and social malaise and get back in gear. The answer to that question is also "Yes." Changes have come so fast since Prime Minister Abe took office that the situation in Japan can be compared to the breakup of a logjam. Even diehard optimists have been surprised.

Fukushima has turned out to be one of many wake-up calls – the others including competition from Korea, Taiwan, and China; China's claims to the Senkaku Islands and the South China Sea; anti-Japanese riots in China; missile tests in North Korea; and a growing awareness that the United States has not lost the battle for high-tech leadership to Asia after all, but has actually retained the lead and regained its earlier momentum. And if we look past the public-opinion polls to the export promotion efforts of the Japanese government and heavy industrial companies, it is apparent that even Japan's faith in nuclear power has not been shaken.

Japan has signed nuclear energy agreements with 14 countries and is pursuing five more (India, Brazil, South Africa, Mexico, and Saudi Arabia). Japanese nuclear power plant builders Hitachi, Toshiba, and MHI have recently won or participated in contracts in Turkey, Vietnam, the United Arab Emirates, Europe, and the United States. In January 2014, Toshiba announced plans to buy 50% of NuGen UK, a joint venture established by GDF Suez and Iberdrola of Spain to build new reactors at Moorside in northern England.

In October 2012, Hitachi acquired nuclear power plant builder Horizon Nuclear Power from German utilities RWE and E.ON, thereby becoming the prime contractor for what is likely to be more than 5,000MW of new generating capacity in the U.K. Hitachi president Hiroaki Nakanishi commented: "I am extremely pleased that we have been successful in acquiring Horizon Nuclear Power. Today starts our 100-year commitment to the U.K. and its vision to achieve a long-term, secure, low-carbon, and affordable energy supply" (Hitachi press release, October 30, 2012).

In September 2014, Hitachi opened its European Nuclear Research Centre in the U.K. According to the company's press release, the purpose of the center is to facilitate the development of safe and efficient nuclear power in Europe based on advanced plant maintenance technology and proven decommissioning techniques, and to contribute to Hitachi's global nuclear power business.

# VI.
# Conclusion: In for the Long Haul

While China grabs the headlines, Japan's international economy continues to expand, driven by the search for new opportunities for growth and technological diversification.

It should be obvious from statistics and the news flow that "dynamic," "adaptable," and "formidable" are more appropriate descriptions of the Japanese economy than "hidebound," "sclerotic," or "irrelevant." Japan's export-driven growth strategy has evolved into a system based on overseas production and acquisition of foreign companies, while protectionism at home is giving way to a combination of comparative advantage and investment incentives aimed at solving structural problems such as over-concentration of economic activity in Tokyo and targeted industries such as healthcare.

By maintaining a large and sophisticated manufacturing base, Japan has also kept unemployment well below American levels and far below European levels. While American unemployment remains stubbornly high and European austerity prevents tens of millions of young people from finding employment, Japan is facing a shortage of workers. Despite being a high-wage manufacturing country, Japan has no structural trade deficit with China. All this raises questions about the fundamental economic assumptions prevalent in the U.S. and Europe.

In the seven decades since WWII, Japan has become an economic insider, a defender of intellectual property rights, and by necessity a strong supporter of the international trade and investment order. As the dominant economic power during that time, the United States greatly assisted Japan's rise to the top of the economic pyramid – both deliberately and inadvertently – and its policies are now doing the same for China. The difference is that Japan is an ally.

As the Asian "economic miracle" spread from Japan to South Korea, Taiwan, Southeast Asia, and China (and as the InfoMercantilist model moved from Japan to South Korea, Taiwan, and China) the same patterns in American behavior were seen again and again. So many jobs have been created in Asia that even limited application of Japanese-type economic policies might have kept America near full employment while preventing the loss of important industries.

Japan does, however, have some severe weaknesses, among them over-reliance on hardware (providing an opportunity for foreign software companies), extreme homogeneity, an inability to get along with Korea and China, and a huge national debt that must be brought under control. In Prime Minister Abe's first two years in office, he and Bank of Japan governor Haruhiko Kuroda got the Japanese economy moving again, but the "hard parts" of Abenomics – economic reform and paying down that debt – start now. The prognosis is reasonably optimistic, but if momentum is lost, the financial situation could become very serious very quickly. It is fortunate for Japan – and a natural consequence of its business model – that it owes most of its debt to itself, and that public-private sector relations are generally cooperative.

Western journalists and economists who regard Japan as feeble or fragile pay insufficient attention to its ability to recover from difficult situations. Tokyo has been totally destroyed twice in the past 100 years – by the Great Kanto Earthquake in 1923 and by American bombing in 1945. In the past few years, the country has had to deal with the Tohoku earthquake and tsunami, the Fukushima nuclear disaster and subsequent shutdown of all Japanese nuclear power plants, and the Thai floods, which severely damaged many Japanese factories and disrupted supply chains all over Asia.

None of this has derailed the Japanese economy. Japan is in for the long haul. It is not a "dying country," and it is not going away. Tough competition from Japanese companies is a basic and permanent feature of the international corporate landscape. Ignoring it simply doesn't make sense.

On November 5, 2013, an assembly of interested persons celebrated the 400th anniversary of the first recorded English roast-beef dinner served in Japan, with a roast-beef dinner of their own, at the Foreign Correspondents Club in Tokyo. The original dinner had been held in honor of Matsura Hoin, who was the *daimyo* (feudal lord) of Hirado, when the British East India Company ship *Clove* arrived there in 1613 to initiate trade with Japan. His direct descendant, 15 generations on, attended the 2013 event.

Today Hitachi, founded in 1910, is planning for its next 100 years – in England. Presumably, there will be another centennial roast beef dinner in 2113.

• • •

*While many observers consider Japan to be in dire economic straits, it is clear that the country remains one of the world's great economic success stories when judged both by objective factors – such as standard of living, unemployment rate, and technological advances – and by the goals of its own highly effective InfoMercantilist business model.*

*With a large share of production, capital, and overall GNP having been moved offshore, Japan today looks more like a modern global corporation than a hide-bound nation unable to adapt to a changing world.*

*Although there are obvious domestic costs inherent to this model (such as the country's large national debt), Japan has achieved export success on a scale wished for, but unmatched by, most other advanced countries. All of this has happened quietly, on the global economic stage – if not in stealth mode, then certainly avoiding the international spotlight, and apparently content in others not recognizing its economic achievements and the fulfillment of its own export-driven agenda.*

*By its own lights, Japan today is a terrific success, and it is time the rest of the world recognize the power and results that have flowed from its perfection of the InfoMercantilist model.*

– Scott Foster

# Bibliography

Anderson, Mark. "SNS Update: Asian Shifts." *Strategic News Service Global Report on Technology and the Economy,* 31 May 2012.

Arase, David. "India-Japan Strategic Partnership in Southeast Asia." *FPRC Journal, 2012 (4),* 2012.

Benioff, Marc. "Why Japan Matters. And Microsoft Doesn't." Salesforce.com, *The CloudBlog,* June 13, 2010. http://cloudblog. salesforce.com/2010/06/why-.html.

Berger, Suzanne, and Ronald Dore, eds. *National Diversity and Global Capitalism.* Ithaca, NY: Cornell University Press, 23 May 1996.

Catan, Thomas. "Japan's Revival Bid Has Global Consequences." *The Wall Street Journal,* 29 July 2013. http://www.wsj.com/articles/ SB10001424127887323971204578629973667666816.

Chellaney, Brahma. "Narendra Modi: India's Shinzo Abe." *The Japan Times,* 20 May, 2014.

Clavell, James. *Shogun.* New York: Delacorte Press, 1 September 1986.

Elkus, Richard J. *Winner Take All: How Competitiveness Shapes the Fate of Nations.* New York: Basic Books, 7 July 2008.

Fingleton, Eamonn. *In Praise of Hard Industries.* New York: Houghton Mifflin Harcourt, 9 September 1999.

Gilder, George. *Microcosm: The Quantum Revolution in Economics and Technology.* New York: Free Press, July 1990.

Grove, Andrew S. *Only the Paranoid Survive: How to Exploit the Crisis Points That Challenge Every Company.* New York: Doubleday Business, 1 September 1996.

Hill, Steven. "The economic fallacy of 'zombie' Japan." *The Guardian*, 11 August 2010. http://www.theguardian.com/commentisfree/cifamerica/2010/aug/11/paul-krugman-japan-lost-decade.

Inagaki, Kana, and Atsuko Fukase. "Cash-Rich Japanese Firms Go on Global Buying Spree." *The Wall Street Journal*, 29 May 2012. http://www.wsj.com/articles/SB10001424052702303505504577403743150818820.

Iwata, Kazumasa et al. *Vision 2050 – Maintain Position as a First-tier Nation*. Tokyo: Japan Center for Economic Research, April 2014. http://www.jcer.or.jp/eng/pub/.

Iwata, Mari. "Fukushima Watch: Draft Plan Sees Minimal Water Risks in 7 Years." *The Wall Street Journal*, 4 December 2013. http://blogs.wsj.com/japanrealtime/2013/12/04/fukushima-watch-draft-plan-sees-minimal-water-risks-in-7-years/.

Johnson, Chalmers. *MITI and the Japanese Miracle: The Growth of Industrial Policy, 1925-1975*. Palo Alto, CA, Stanford University Press, 1 June 1982.

Johnstone, Bob. *Brilliant! Shuji Nakamura and the Revolution in Lighting Technology*. Amherst, NY: Prometheus Books, 2007.

Johnstone, Bob. *We Were Burning: Japanese Entrepreneurs and the Forging of the Electronic Age*. New York: Basic Books, 1998.

Kallender-Umezu, Paul. "Japan, Vietnam Sign Deal for Two Radar Imaging Satellites." *SpaceNews*, 4 November 2011. http://spacenews.com/japan-vietnam-sign-deal-two-radar-imaging-satellites.

Kato, Yasuhiro et al. "Deep-sea mud in the Pacific Ocean as a potential resource for rare-earth elements." *Nature Geoscience 4.8* (2011): 535-539.

Katz, Richard. "Voodoo Abenomics: Japan's Failed Comeback Plan." New York: *Foreign Affairs*, July/August 2014.

Kawasaki, Ichiro. *Japan Unmasked*. North Clarendon, VT: Charles E. Tuttle Co., 1969. (Out of print.)

Kikuchi, Makoto. *Japanese Electronics: A Worm's Eye View of Its Evolution.* Tokyo: The Simul Press, 1983.

Kiyosawa, Yoshihide. "A Message from the Head of R&D." *Harmonic Drive Systems Inc.* https://www.hds.co.jp/english/development/policy/message/.

Mauldin, John. "What Has QE Actually Accomplished?" *Outside the Box,* 20 August 2013. http://www.mauldineconomics.com/outsidethebox/what-has-qe-actually-accomplished.

METI (Minister of Economy, Trade and Industry, Japan). "Launching International Feasibility Studies on the 'Smart Community' Concept." Press release, March 2012. http://www.meti.go.jp/english/press/2012/0312_02.html.

Nakamura, Shuji, Stephen Pearton, and Gerhard Fasol. *The Blue Laser Diode: The Complete Story.* Berlin; New York: Springer, 1997.

Prestowitz, Clyde. *The Betrayal of American Prosperity: Free Market Delusions, America's Decline, and How We Must Compete in the Post-Dollar Era.* New York: Free Press, 11 May 2010.

Railway-technology.com. "California High-Speed Rail Network, United States of America." Undated. http://www.railway-technology.com/projects/california/.

Schuman, Michael. "One Last Chance for Japan." *TIME,* 4 December 2014. http://time.com/3617926/one-last-chance-for-japan/.

Sekiguchi, Toko. "PM Abe Shows Off Hawkish Stance, Pop-Culture Knowledge." *The Wall Street Journal,* 27 September 2013. http://blogs.wsj.com/japanrealtime/2013/09/27/pm-abe-shows-off-hawkish-stance-pop-culture-knowledge/.

Smith, Nicholas. "Japan Strategy: Earnings in the fast lane." Hong Kong: *CLSA,* February 2015.

Soble, Jonathan, and Ben McLannahan. "Japan's Shinzo Abe reveals tax plan as business confidence soars." *Financial Times,* 1 October 2013. http://www.ft.com/intl/cms/s/0/960485b0-2a2f-11e3-bbb8-00144feab7de.html.

Stiglitz, Joseph. Quoted in "New BoJ chief pledges 'all-out efforts' on deflation." *Agence France-Presse*, 21 May 2013.

Tasker, Peter. "Austin Powers on Abenomics." *Peter Tasker* (online), 21 August 2013. http://www.petertasker.asia/reflections/austin-powers-on-abenomics/.

Todd, Emmanuel. "The paradox of America's fading empire." *Nikkei Asian Review*, 16 January 2014. http://asia.nikkei.com/magazine/20140116-Reading-2014/Viewpoints/The-paradox-of-Americas-fading-empire.

Toshiba Middle East. "The Origins of Toshiba." *Toshiba Middle East*, undated. http://www.toshibamea.com/en/the-origins-of-toshiba.

Tsuru, Shigeto. *Japan's Capitalism: Creative Defeat and Beyond.* New York: Cambridge University Press, 1996.

Unattributed. "Shrinking Japan eyes ambitious population target." *Nikkei Asian Review*, 14 May 2014. http://asia.nikkei.com/Politics-Economy/Policy-Politics/Shrinking-Japan-eyes-ambitious-population-target.

Wolf, Martin, Jonathan Soble, and David Pilling. "Transcript of interview with Haruhiko Kuroda, governor of the Bank of Japan." *Financial Times*, 3 January 2014. http://www.ft.com/intl/cms/s/0/f1e46c46-7472-11e3-9125-00144feabdco.html.

# Acknowledgments

First of all, I would like to thank Mark Anderson, founder and CEO of Strategic News Service (SNS) and Chairman of the SNS Future in Review (FiRe) conference; and Sally Anderson, SNS Editor-in-Chief and Production Manager. Without their support, creating this book would not have been possible. I would also like to thank the rest of the team at SNS and participants in the FiRe conferences over the years, including John Petote, Lee Hall, Ty Carlson, Thomas Curran, Sidney Rittenberg, and many others.

In addition, I have received a great deal of information and many insights from Richard Elkus, Nobuo Hatta, Ed Brogan, Anita Killian, Kunihiko Nakade, Masaru Tamamoto, David Arase, William Saito, Jonathan Epstein, Nicholas Smith, Peter Tasker, Peter Wolff, Christopher Holes, Jeff Bahrenburg, Ben Moyer, Matt Aizawa, Yashwant Bajaj, Akira Yamauchi, Takakatsu Sano, Tait Ratcliffe, Thomas Zengage, Michiyo Nakamoto, Alexandra Harney, Paul Kallender-Umezu, Yumiko Foster, Tadahiko Shimazu of Hamamatsu Photonics, Hajime Kinoshita of NEC, Kazunori Yagi of Yokogawa Electric, Naoyuki Nakayama of Chiyoda Corp., Hiroharu Katogi of Minebea, Masu Wakabayashi of Optex, Tom Tsuneishi of Tokyo Electron Laboratories, Tsunesaburo Uemura of Nikon, Takayuki Usumi of ULVAC, Tetsuya Iizuka of THine Electronics, Osamu Tsuji of SAMCO, Masahiro Nagayasu of Nidec, and numerous other friends, associates, and company representatives in Japan.

# About the Author

Scott Foster is a research analyst and writer who worked for American and European investment banks in Japan and Korea for more than 25 years. He is currently Partner at TAP Japan, an investment consultancy in Tokyo, and Alliance Partner at Translink Corporate Finance, a multinational investment banking group headquartered in Europe. Scott is Asia editor of the Strategic News Service (SNS) Global Report, author of the quarterly SNS Asia Letter, and a member of the SNS Future in Review (FiRe) conference advisory board. He holds an MA from the Johns Hopkins University School of Advanced International Studies (1982), a first-degree black belt from the Karate-no-Michi World Federation (KWF), and an instructor's (*shihan*) license from the Tozan-ryu school of *shakuhachi* (end-blown Japanese bamboo flute) music.

# Index

www.ingramcontent.com/pod-product-compliance
Lightning Source LLC
Chambersburg PA
CBHW061311220326
41599CB00026B/4828